AN IDIO
TO THE BOOK

GW01033520

Joanne D Cameron

i

AN IDIOT'S GUIDE
TO THE BOOK OF REVELATION

Joanne D Cameron

First published in 2020 by KAD Publishing

240 Bounces Road, London N9 8LA

Copyright © 2020 Joanne D Cameron

Record of this book is available from the British Library.

Cover design by Fady Gremesty

ISBN 978-1-9160249-4-6

Dedicated to Anthony
My Husband, Priest and Lover

Table of Contents

Illustrations by Guy Chapman

Acknowledgements

Writing this book has brought a great amount of joy to my life. Embarking on a project that is just beyond your capabilities brings an experience that enhances confidence, self-worth and self-esteem. And therefore, I have gained much more than I have given in putting this work together.

Having said that, I must say, books do not come about through the efforts of one person. So many people gave invaluable assistance that allowed this book to be written, and who need to be acknowledged.

First, I must thank Dr Keith Davidson, a life-long friend, who put the thought into my head that I could be an author.

Also, thank you to KAD Publishing for viewing this book (and its companion) as worthy of being published.

Having taken on this project, I now realise just how valuable family members are in my life. My sister Claudia (an author herself), has always led the way and confirmed that the path was safe to travel. My daughter, Kelly, and her husband, Olawale Aliowe, were always enthusiastic in reading my drafts and giving feedback that kept me on track. My younger daughter, Sophie, who can always be trusted to be brutally honest in her opinions (a chip off the old block). My son-in-law, Pastor Jonathan Holder, who was kind enough to read, and give an expert opinion and helpful tips.

I would also like to thank my long-time friend Mervyn Weir, who helped me understand the worth of my penmanship.

And of course, I must pay tribute to the illustrator of all the drawings in this book, Guy Chapman. In our search for a suitable artist, we came across Guy's work. Not only is Guy a marvellous artist, he is also a Christian, which proved important in grasping the religious concepts that enabled Revelation's textual descriptions to be translated into thought provoking images. Guy produced his unique work through prayer, experience, humour, and a meticulous sense of detail. His illustrations can be studied again and again, as there will always be some feature you missed – I promise, the more you look, the more you will see.

Last but not least, I must acknowledge Anthony, my rock, who just happens to be my husband. He must take pride of place in the list of all those I have looked to for support during the writing of this book. I have doubted my abilities, many times, but he has never been in doubt. He has kept me writing when I wanted to throw everything out of the window. Because I know he loves me, I have believed his words of encouragement, and kept going. I don't think he knows just how instrumental he has been in the completion of this project.

As a Christian, it is imperative that I give thanks to God for inspiring me to write this book. The original text (the book of Revelation as found in The Holy Bible) came from Him. And my feeble attempts to make His book more accessible to 'Joe Public' was done on His instruction, and by His step-by-step leading. May it bring glory to His name, and afford its readers an opportunity to get to know God, the Creator of the universe.

Joanne D Cameron

Foreword

Dear Reader,

Thank you for opening this book.

It is written as a companion to my first book 'An Idiot's Guide to the Book of Daniel', which you will find referenced throughout. The books of Daniel and Revelation complement one another and help interpret each other. Therefore, if you haven't already read my book on Daniel, I hope you will be encouraged to do so after reading its companion.

My reason for writing this book is simply to help ordinary non-intellectuals (like myself) understand the book of Revelation. I have delivered Revelation Seminars for the public and conducted Daniel and Revelation Studies for years, and always get a thrill out of witnessing the students progressively gain in-depth knowledge of the prophetic messages. This book is for anyone who is curious about Bible prophecies but feel the prophetic books are beyond their understanding. And, if you are a fan of history, you will also be amazed at the historical references and events that back-up Bible prophecy.

As well as the prophecies, you will learn about the writer of Revelation, John, Jesus' disciple. John faithfully recorded all that was shown to him, but was largely unaware of the meaning of the visions he was describing, the majority of which he would not live to see fulfilled. But, we who live in the 21st century are able to look back and see how the visions have been realised, and look forward to the fulfilment of those yet to take place.

My main source has been the book of Revelation (New International Version). Other Biblical references are also included to support explanations and interpretations. These supportive Bible texts are for your information, so you can choose to look them up, or not, as you wish. Additional sources are referenced and included in the book's bibliography.

People have asked me about the title of this book. Personally, I love step-by-step instruction manuals (in other words, the 'Idiot Guide') that transport me from ignorance to expertise. I hope you will come to view this work in the same way and not feel insulted by its title. We will journey through the book of Revelation verse by verse, giving explanations as we go. At the end of it all, you should understand every verse. Don't be afraid to read chapters more than once. If you are not used to deciphering prophetic symbols, you may wish to proceed slowly and purposefully. This book has been written in plain, simple English because it is important for you to understand its themes and messages. I promise you will find something in them that will impact your life.

Revelation is an exciting book, full of colourful imagery and memorable characters from the past, present and future. You may find, at the end of your reading, your perspective on God, the universe and everything, has changed.

The mind blowing illustrations of Guy Chapman have been included to stimulate your imagination even further, as we embark on this Biblical extravaganza.

I hope you enjoy the journey.

Joanne D Cameron

Revelation Chapter One

INTRODUCTIONS, INTRODUCTIONS, INTRODUCTIONS

Based on Revelation 1:1-20

The book of Revelation is an interesting and exciting book; often thought of as the most mysterious and frightening of all the books in the Bible. Yet, its very name tells us that it wants to be understood. It is a book of revelations. It is actually a love letter from Jesus to His church throughout the ages. He is seeking to reveal Himself to His people and guide them safely into His eternal kingdom.

As we will see, the book is full of mysteries but it is not mysterious. Some of the images look frightening but the book itself is encouraging. Revelation is the church's road map from the AD90s to the creation of the New Earth. It is a book full of symbols, but the explanation for each symbol is found within the Bible. Therefore, we have all we need to understand this wonderful prophetic book.

It was John, the beloved disciple of Jesus, who wrote the book of Revelation around AD90. The first chapter is an introduction, and within it, more and more introductions unfold.

Revelation 1:1-2 - tell us that although John is writing the book, it is truly a revelation from Jesus Christ Himself. John further states the book is a prophetic chain letter, for it originated with God the Father, who passed it to Jesus, who sent it via His angel, who showed it to John. John merely wrote down what he saw, and he confirms that indeed it is the word of God and the testimony of Jesus Christ. We are going to learn a great deal about the character of Jesus. We will see Him in different roles, portrayed in different images, and named with many names. The testimony is not only from Him, it is also about Him. And, throughout the book it will be confirmed over and over again that we can trust its message because it is of divine origin: all that we learn from this revelation is true.

Already, we have reason to be excited: John was shown visions of the present and the future, and he faithfully recorded everything he saw so we can know God's will for His church.

Revelation 1:3 – John pronounces a blessing on everyone who becomes conversant with the book of Revelation. They are blessed if they read it aloud for others to hear, and they are blessed if they hear it being read and take it to heart. This certainly doesn't sound like a book that is mysterious beyond comprehension. No, God wants us to understand it. John then says the time for the book's fulfilment is near. Therefore, the prophecies of the book will soon begin to take place.

Revelation 1:4-5 – The book of Revelation begins in the form of letters. Its first three chapters are addressed to the *"seven churches in the province of Asia"*, namely, Ephesus; Smyrna; Pergamum; Thyatira; Sardis; Philadelphia; Laodicea. Seven literal churches existing in John's time.

At the beginning of each letter, John introduces himself, identifies to whom he is writing, pronounces a blessing on the churches from the Godhead; God the Father *"who is, and who was, and who is to come"*, the Holy Spirit (described as the sevenfold Spirit), and Jesus Christ *"who is the faithful witness, the firstborn from the dead, and the ruler of the kings of the earth."* Notice that John is introducing the Godhead, not only by naming them, but by describing each with a characteristic that identifies their divinity. God the Father is described as being eternal; always existent. The Holy Spirit is *"sevenfold"*. Here is our introduction to the significance of numbers in Revelation. In this book, seven is the number of perfection (as is the number twelve). We are going to come across a lot of sevens and twelves in our study. They will always signify spiritual perfection or completeness. So here, John is describing the Holy Spirit as perfect, or the Author of perfection.

There are different theories on number symbolism in the Bible. Here is one guide to consider:

Number	Symbolic of:
One	The one true God
Two	Witnessing (the disciples were sent out two-by-two)
Three	The Godhead (Father, Son, and Holy Spirit)
Four	Mankind (the one created by the Godhead)
Five	The grace of God
Six	Evil (falling short of perfection)
Seven	Spiritual perfection or completeness (the Godhead (3) working on mankind (4): 3+4)
Twelve	Spiritual perfection or completeness (the Godhead (3) working on mankind (4): 3x4)

Revelation 1:5-6 - Jesus is introduced in greater detail than the other persons of the Godhead. Not surprising, as John knows Him personally. Jesus is credited as the *"faithful witness"*; again, we can believe His testimony, but also, whilst He was here on earth, living as a man, John saw for himself Jesus' faithful witness of His heavenly Father. He authentically portrayed the character of God (see John 14:7,10,11). Jesus is also *"the firstborn from the dead"*. His resurrection was personally experienced by John. He saw the risen Christ, ate and fellowshipped with Him, was instructed by Him, and witnessed His ascension. John also knows that Jesus is the *"ruler of the kings of the earth"* for, at Jesus' ascension angels confirmed to the watching disciples that Jesus would return, this time as King of kings (see Acts 1:11). This knowledge must have been especially comforting to John as he was now being kept in exile by a king of the earth.

John then outlines the entire plan of salvation: Jesus is our Saviour; He loves us; shed His blood to save us from sin; and has therefore made all who accept Him, "*a kingdom of priests to serve his God and Father*". John is comparing all who personally accept Jesus as their Sacrifice, to ancient Israel, the literal kingdom of priests. Therefore, because we have accepted Jesus, we are spiritual Israel; God's chosen nation.

Then, John is overwhelmed and utters praise to God:

"*to him be glory and power for ever and ever! Amen*".

Indeed, when we consider all that Jesus has done for mankind, where He found us in our sinful state, helpless, hopeless and doomed to everlasting death, how He saved us, and where He has taken us, shouldn't we also join with John in declaring glory and praise to our Saviour, Creator and King? To know God is to love and honour Him forever. Amen!

Revelation 1:7 – John reminds us that Jesus will be coming back to earth. He sees the event and points us to it. He says "*Look, he is coming with the clouds*". As we know that when Jesus returns to earth He will be accompanied by all the angels of heaven (see Matthew 25:31), we can assume that when John describes Jesus as coming with the clouds, this is how myriads of angels appear when travelling as a throng. When Jesus ascended to heaven, "*a cloud hid him from their sight*" (Acts 1:9). It seems these clouds of angels travel with Jesus as He ascends from, or descends to, earth.

In his vision of the coming of Jesus, John points out this will be no secret event, "*every eye will see him*". Notice, John does not say that every sighted person will see Jesus, but *every* eye. Even the blind will witness the advent of Christ, and, we will all see Him at the same time. Jesus, Himself warned that we should not believe anyone telling us to go here or there to see His second coming. It will be a spectacle that lights up the sky from east to west (see

Matthew 24:26, 27). No-one will have to tell us that Jesus has returned; we will all see the event for ourselves.

But, John says another group of people will witness the event: the soldiers who drove nails through Jesus' hands and feet. These soldiers are of course long dead. How will they see the Second Coming? At His trial, presided over by Caiaphas, the High Priest, Jesus warned Caiaphas that he would be raised up to see Jesus come back to earth in all His glory (see Matthew 26:64). Then in Daniel 12:2, we are told of a partial resurrection of the wicked that will take place when Jesus comes. This is a mini-resurrection specifically for Caiaphas and those involved in crucifying Jesus. They will be raised to see Jesus, not as their beaten, battered and bruised prisoner but as King of kings and Lord of lords. No wonder the book of Daniel says they will suffer *"shame and everlasting contempt."* (Daniel 12:2)

In Revelation 1:7, John makes it clear that it is not only Caiaphas and the Roman soldiers who will grieve at Jesus' return; there will be others. John states *"all peoples on earth"* will mourn too. It is clear that for the majority of people living on earth the Second Coming will be an unwelcomed event. Most people will be unprepared and taken unawares. To them, Jesus' coming will be a harbinger of doom and utter disaster. What a sad picture. Even though each person has been given every opportunity to give their hearts to Jesus and be saved, the majority of the earth's population will decide to reject the invitation, and so effectively choose their own destruction (see Matthew 7:13,14). John confirms, *"So shall it be! Amen"* (Revelation 1:7).

Revelation 1:8 – Then, God introduces Himself as the Alpha and Omega, the One who is, was, and will be; the Almighty. In other words, God who has always existed, exists now, and will exist forever, the all-powerful and everlasting.

There is the introduction to the book of Revelation. All the protagonists are present: God the Father; God the Son; God the Holy Spirit; the holy angel who will show the visions, and John the Revelator, the recorder of the visions.

Now we are ready to begin.

Revelation 1:9 – John now introduces himself as one of the brethren. He is writing his letters to the brethren of the seven churches, and identifies with them. He is just an ordinary brother in Christ. He does not see himself as special in any way, even though he has been blessed with receiving this prophetic message from God. He is like them; a sinner saved by the grace of God. However, he is suffering for his faith. John was sent in exile to the Greek island of Patmos by the Roman Emperor, Domitian, as punishment for preaching the gospel. John was now in his nineties, yet he was subjected to excruciating torture. According to Foxe's 'Book of Martyrs', John was plunged into a vat of boiling oil in front of the Colosseum, on the orders of Domitian. John miraculously survived this ordeal, and Domitian, fearful that the elderly apostle could not be killed, exiled him to hard labour in the mines of Patmos. It was here that John received his visions.

Remarkably, John did not end his days on Patmos. A later emperor pardoned him, and he was able to resume his preaching of the gospel in Ephesus. It is said, John was the only disciple who did not die a martyr. He died of natural causes in his late nineties. (www.deedsofgod.com)

Revelation 1:10 – John reports that he received his first vision on *"the Lord's Day"*. Which day is this? Jesus identifies the Lord's day as the Sabbath (see Matthew 12:8), and this is confirmed in the Old Testament when God says *"But the seventh day is the Sabbath of the Lord thy God . . ."* (Exodus 20:10 KJV). Therefore, John received his first vision on the Sabbath day (Saturday; the seventh day of the week).

John describes his condition as being *"in the Spirit"*. This was clearly no ordinary dream; John was being directed by the Holy Spirit. 2 Peter 1:21 tells us the method used by God to give prophetic messages to His prophets is through the moving of the Holy Spirit. John is therefore confirming that God is the originator of his writings.

Revelation 1:10-11 - John hears a voice behind him, which sounds like a trumpet. This must be the voice of God for it says: *"I am Alpha and Omega, the first and the last"*. This is indeed God who instructs John to write on a scroll whatever he sees, and send it to the seven churches in Asia.

Revelation 1:12 – John is curious; he wants to see what God looks like. He turns, and sees seven golden lampstands (or candlesticks). The lampstands are identified in Revelation 1:20 as symbolising the seven churches.

Revelation 1:13-16 – Walking amongst the seven golden candlesticks John sees a human-like figure, and here is His description:

- He is wearing a floor-length robe;
- He has a golden breastplate;
- His hair is white like wool, and white as snow;
- His eyes blaze like fire
- His feet look like polished brass
- His voice sounds like flowing waters
- In His right hand He is carrying seven stars. (Here we have the number seven again, that is, spiritual completeness). In Revelation 1:20 the seven stars are identified as being symbolic of the angels of the seven churches. In the book of Revelation, we will see that sometimes angels are interchangeable with human messengers of God. Angels are certainly God's messengers; they exist to do God's bidding (see Hebrews 1:14). In Revelation we will also find that, especially when it comes to spreading the gospel, no distinction is made between heavenly messengers and earthly messengers. Therefore, earthly messengers who carry out the work of

spreading the gospel are called angels. Moreover, the Greek word used here is 'angelos' which means 'messenger' whether human or heavenly. Hence, the seven angels (seven stars) of the seven churches could well refer to the spiritual leaders of the seven churches to whom John was to send his letters.

- He has a sharp two-edged sword in His mouth. In Hebrews 4:12 the word of God is described as a two-edged sword that cuts asunder and is a discerner of the thoughts of the heart. It is clear this human-like figure speaks the powerful word of God.
- His face shines like the sun shining at full strength.

Revelation 1:17-18 - John recognises the figure immediately. He realises he is in the presence of the Son of God. John is overwhelmed, and faints. Daniel reacted in the same manner when he saw Jesus at the Tigris River. He also fainted (see Daniel 10:9).

Jesus revives John and tells him not to be afraid. If there was any doubt, this imposing figure identifies Himself as Jesus. He says:

- *"I am the First and the Last"* – I am God;
- *"I am the Living One; I was dead, and now look, I am alive for ever and ever"* – I am Jesus who died for the sins of the world, but I am also the resurrected Lord who will never die again;
- *"And I hold the keys of death and Hades"* – Because I conquered death, I am qualified to determine who will suffer the second death in hell fire. In other words, those who follow Me will never experience the second death (the death from which there is no return); they will live with Me forever.

Revelation 1:19-20 – Jesus instructs John to write down everything he is about to be shown, which will be prophecies of events to come.

Jesus then identifies the seven stars as the messengers of the seven churches, and the seven golden lampstands as the seven churches (as shown above).

Let us consider, for a moment, where Jesus is standing as He gives His message to John. The seven golden lampstands that symbolise the seven churches, are familiar objects to John. In Exodus 25:31-40 we see the instructions given by God to Moses for the making of the golden lampstand to be situated in the wilderness sanctuary. The wilderness sanctuary and everything in it were made exactly as instructed by God. He gave Moses the blueprint and told him to follow it to the smallest detail. The lampstand was made up of seven lamps that burned continuously in the first compartment of the sanctuary, known as the Holy Place (see Exodus 27:20-21, Hebrews 9:2). Then in Hebrews 8:1-6 we are told that the wilderness sanctuary was a copy of the heavenly sanctuary.

Therefore, there is a sanctuary or temple in heaven that the wilderness sanctuary and subsequent Jewish temple were modelled on. Hebrews 9:11 further tells us that Jesus is our High Priest who officiates in the heavenly temple on our behalf. In Revelation 1:12,13, when we see Jesus in heaven walking amidst the seven golden lampstands, we can safely conclude that Jesus is in the first compartment of the heavenly temple (the Holy Place), and this is where He begins His testimony.

Later in Revelation we will see the action move from the Holy Place to the Most Holy Place which will be hugely significant in identifying where we are in earth's history, and Jesus' ministry.

This ends the preface to the book of Revelation. What an introduction. I cannot think of a more dramatic way of introducing a book. Everything we have witnessed so far points to an exciting ride.

Revelation Chapter Two

EPHESUS, SMYRNA, PERGAMUM AND THYATIRA

Based on Revelation 2:1-29

Revelation chapters two and three are the letters to the seven churches in Asia. These letters are dictated by Jesus.

Before we go into the letters, let us explore their application. The message for each church clearly goes beyond commendations, instructions and admonitions to single churches. Bible scholars generally believe each message can be applied in the following three ways:

- a message to the literal Asian church;
- a message to God's church during a specific historical era;
- a message to each child of God.

The format of all seven letters to the churches follows a similar pattern:

- The church is identified;
- Jesus introduces Himself to the church in a meaningful way, using descriptions attributed to Him in Revelation chapter one;
- Jesus commends the church;
- Jesus criticises the church;
- Jesus warns what will happen if the church does not repent of its wrong doing;
- Jesus admonishes the church to pay attention to the warning;
- Jesus promises a heavenly reward.

The message to the church in Ephesus

Revelation 2:1 – The church of Ephesus is identified, and John is instructed to write to the "*angel*" or leader of the church. The fact that John is to write to the angel of the church adds weight to the explanation that the angels of the churches are actually the human church leaders, as John would be unable to write to an angel.

Jesus identifies Himself as the one who "*holds the seven stars in his right hand and walks among the seven golden lampstands.*" It would, no doubt, have been very comforting for the church members to understand that Jesus walks among His churches. He does not leave them alone but is constantly with them, directing their leaders: He cares for them.

Revelation 2:2-3 – Jesus commends the Ephesus church for its "*hard work and perseverance*". It does not tolerate wicked people. It tests those who come to the church claiming to be apostles of Jesus, to see if they are true or false. It has endured hardships for Jesus' name and has not grown weary.

This commendation goes beyond the literal church for it also applies to the era of the apostolic church (AD31 – AD100), set up after Jesus' ascension. This was the church written about in 'Acts of the Apostles'; the church of James (the brother of Jesus), Peter and the other disciples, and of course Paul. This was indeed a church that was hard working and untiring. It spread the gospel to the then known world (see Colossians 1:23), and suffered great oppression for its efforts. This church vigorously sought to keep its message pure and free from false doctrine (see Galatians 1:8,9).

Revelation 2:4 – However, Jesus warns the church that its focus is slipping. It has lost its first love; its faithfulness to Jesus is being diluted and its adherence to the truth is wavering.

Revelation 2:5 – Jesus admonishes the church to consider how far it has fallen and, to repent and return to carrying out its past actions. He warns that if the church continues on its present path, its lampstand will be removed from its place. In other words, if it does not amend its ways Jesus will reject the church. A serious warning indeed. Here, Jesus is not only warning the church in Ephesus, but also the Apostolic Church (AD31 – AD100). This church, began as a dynamic, evangelistic movement; spreading the pure gospel of Jesus Christ throughout the known world. However, it underwent some drastic changes as it experienced the infiltration of 'strange' doctrine. As a consequence, by AD120 we see a very different Christian church.

Revelation 2:6 – Nevertheless, Jesus does commend the Ephesus church. He praises it for hating the practices of the Nicolaitans, as He does. Today, there are differing views regarding the beliefs of the Nicolaitans, but as their name can be translated from the Greek as 'let-us-eat-ers', it is generally thought their religious services included sexual immorality and the sacrificing of food to idols. (www.weekly.israelbiblecentre.com/who-were-nicolaitans) In the book of Acts, we find the Apostolic church specifically instructing new converts to abstain from these two practices (see Acts 15:22-29). And in Revelation, Jesus confirms His hatred of Nicolaitan teachings.

Revelation 2:7 - Jesus states: "*Whoever has ears, let them hear what the Spirit says to the churches.*" This was a common phrase used by Jesus whilst on earth in order to draw His hearers' attention to the importance of His message, for example, in the parable of the farmer sowing seed in diverse soils (see Matthew 13:1-9). Jesus is saying 'listen carefully, I am speaking about how you must be saved.'

Jesus then goes on to highlight the heavenly reward awaiting His children who endure to the end. "*To the one who is victorious, I will give the right to eat from the Tree of Life which is in the paradise of God.*" In the Bible, we first see the Tree of Life in the Garden of Eden (see Genesis 2:8). However, mankind lost access to this life-perpetuating tree when Adam and Eve sinned (see Genesis 3:24). Jesus now promises that His victorious people, who keep Him as their focus, will once again be allowed to eat from the Tree of Life, and so attain immortality.

This is clearly a promise not only to the literal church of Ephesus, and the church of the apostolic era, but to God's children through all ages. We all need to keep Jesus as our first love; refuse to follow after false doctrine; and live in harmony with the Ten Commandments through the guidance of the Holy Spirit. This is how we become victorious and, when Jesus returns, gain eternal life.

The message to the church in Smyrna

Revelation 2:8 – John is instructed to write to the leader of the church in Smyrna. Jesus identifies Himself as the letter's Author and "... *the First and Last, who died and came to life again.*" Only Jesus can fit this description.

Revelation 2:9 – Jesus knows the condition of all His churches. He identifies the Smyrna church as afflicted and poor. No doubt the literal Smyrna church of John's time saw both poverty and affliction, but the Smyrna historical era for Christians was certainly one of great persecution and privation (AD100 – AD313). Indeed, historically this is known as the period of the Persecuted Church when the rigorous pursuit and massacre of Christians greatly increased during the reign of the Roman emperors. Nevertheless, Jesus calls the Smyrna church *"rich"*. Therefore, the church, whilst enduring the harshest of treatments, was rich towards God; laying up spiritual treasure in heaven. It is interesting that the Smyrna church receives no censure from Jesus. The maltreatment it suffered kept it true to the gospel and, consequently, attracted thousands of converts.

Jesus says, this church will be slandered by false Christians, led by the devil, in his attempt to dismantle the church of God from the inside.

Revelation 2:10 – Jesus admonishes His church not to be afraid of the coming persecution, which although ordered by human rulers is in reality choreographed by the devil. Some of Jesus' followers will be imprisoned, and this persecution will last *"ten days"*.

This time period (ten days) introduces us to one of the rules of prophecy, namely the 'day/year principle'. In Revelation, this principle is used when time periods are shown in prophecy. The rule is:

One prophetic day = One literal year

The rationale for this principle is found in two Bible texts - Numbers 14:34 and Ezekiel 4:6 where God gives two time prophecies, and instructs *"a day for each year"*.

Using this rule we can interpret the ten prophetic days, referred to by Jesus in Revelation 2L10, as ten literal years of persecution. The question we must now ask is, were there ten years of persecution during the Smyrna period? The answer is, yes.

". . . during the reign of emperor Diocletian from AD303 – AD313 the desire was to remove Christianity from the empire and thus preserve the Roman way of life, which he believed was under threat by the monumental growth of the Christian religion. Diocletian's first decree in AD303 was to ban Christianity throughout the empire, plus to burn all Christian religious books including the Bible. This unleashed an unmitigated and relentless persecution of Christians in the entire empire." (www.revelationbibleprophecy.org/revelation2)

Jesus warns that the persecution may even lead to death. Nevertheless, He encourages the church to remain faithful, because death is not the end for His faithful ones; they will gain eternal life and a victor's crown.

Revelation 2:11 – *"Whoever has ears, let them hear what the Spirit says to the churches."* Again, Jesus is admonishing His people to pay attention to the message, which comes through the direction of the Holy Spirit. And here is Jesus' promise of eternal reward: *"The one who is victorious will not be hurt at all by the second death."*

This is surely a message not only for the persecuted Smyrna church members, and martyrs from the historical Smyrna period, but also to all Jesus' followers. We may indeed suffer persecution, and even death, for our faith, but the first death is not the death we must fear. Mankind is mortal, and because of sin we must all die the first death (see Romans 6:23), but we need not suffer the second death, that is, the eternal death from which no-one comes back (see Revelation 20:6). What assurance for the martyrs; their eternal lives are safe in Christ Jesus. How comforting for us also!

The message to the church in Pergamum

Revelation 2:12 – Jesus introduces Himself to the church of Pergamum as *". . . Him who has the sharp, double-edged sword"*. As we saw in Revelation chapter one Jesus is identifying Himself as the Word of God (see also John 1:1). Jesus is the fulfilment of the Bible. He cuts through our bodies and penetrates our innermost being with His truth.

Revelation 2:13 – Jesus has great commendation for Pergamum. The church is situated where Satan's throne is, yet it has remained faithful to Jesus. It has not renounced its faith, even though Jesus' faithful witness, Antipas, was put to death in the city (where the devil also lives).

The historical Pergamum period was AD313 – AD538. This period covers the continued rule of the Roman Empire, and its transformation into the religious power, Papal Rome. The book of Revelation will return to this power and its effect on the true church of God, again and again. However, at this point, Pergamum, which is under the rule of Rome, is identified as situated *". . . where Satan has his throne"*.

(Please see the quotation below from 'The Seven Epistles of Christ', Taylor G Brunch, pages 149-150, to see the sequence of events that link Pergamum with Rome and Satan's throne.)

"*When Cyrus captured the city of Babylon, the ancient seat of Satan's counterfeit system of religion, the supreme pontiff of the Chaldean mysteries and his retinue of priests fled from the city and ultimately made their residence in Pergamos. Here they re-established their Babylonian worship and made the kings of Pergamum the chief pontiffs of their religion. When Attalus III, the last of the priest-kings, died in 133BC, he bequeathed both his royal and priestly offices to the Romans. A century later, both Julius and Augustus Caesar became emperors of Rome and Pontifex Maximus religious leader of the empire. He was given divine honours, which he handed down to his successors (later rejected by the Christian emperor Gratian AD380). These were later assumed by the popes (firstly by Pope Damasus, thus its transferral to the Church of Rome), the supreme pontiffs of ecclesiastical Rome. Thus Pergamos became the connecting link between the two Babylons, the ancient and the modern. The papal system is patterned after that of Babylon and Rome. This is another reason for the statement of Jesus that Pergamos was the place where Satan dwelleth.*"

Going back to Revelation 2:13, it is generally thought that the putting to death of *"Antipas, my faithful witness"* during the Pergamum period refers to the martyrdom of God's people (not one man) at that time who faithfully witnessed for Christ. The killing of Christians continued throughout the Pergamum era, and the meaning of the name Antipas can be broken down into two words – 'anti' meaning in opposition to, and 'pas' (short for Papas) meaning father or pope. Therefore, the 'faithful witness Antipas' are all those who opposed the Church of Rome during the Pergamum era and were martyred for their beliefs.

Revelation 2:14 – Unfortunately, Jesus is not altogether pleased with the church of Pergamum. He has a few things against it. The church is tolerating false doctrine in its midst: the teaching of Balaam. The sad story of Balaam is found in the book of Numbers in the Old Testament (see Numbers 22-24). Balaam was a false prophet, once true to God, but his love of wealth turned him away from the truth. Balaam was hired by Balak, king of Moab, to curse the Children of Israel as they travelled through the plains of Moab. King Balak was frightened of the Jews, he had heard how they destroyed other nations on their journey, and he was fearful they would do the same to his kingdom. As a result, he engaged Balaam to cast magic spells against them. Balaam tried his best to put curses on God's people but each time he tried, blessings came out of his mouth instead. He then resorted to another plan. He advised king Balak to send beautiful Moabite women into the camp of the Children of Israel to entice the Israelite men into illicit sexual relations. The plan worked, and the men also followed the women in their worship of idols. (See Numbers 25:1-9 and Numbers 31:15-16). This was a dark and dismal episode in the life of God's people; 24,000 of them died as a result.

It is clear God detested the teaching of Balaam which was, the joining of God's people with non-believers in their practices against the true God. In other words, compromising with evil.

Revelation 2:15 – The religion of the Moabites mirrored the pagan Nicolaitan sect. In the message to Ephesus, Jesus commended the church for not allowing the practices of the Nicolaitans to contaminate its doctrine. However, during the Pergamum era, we find the Nicolaitans infiltrating the church.

Revelation 2:16 – Jesus admonishes the Pergamum church to repent. He warns that if they do not, He *". . . will fight against them with the sword of His mouth."* The Word of God will rightly condemn a church that does not uphold the whole truth of God. Moreover, as individuals, we must be careful to follow the teachings of the Bible only, and not compromise with the ideologies, theories and practices of the world. For, as surely as the Children of Israel were led to their deaths through their tolerance of Moabite practices, so we will ultimately be led to eternal death, if we dilute the truth with practices forbidden by the Bible.

Revelation 2:17 – Jesus says again, 'This message is important. You need to hear and understand it.' He promises to His people who are victorious over spiritual compromise, *". . . the hidden manna . . . and a white stone with a new name written on it, known only to the one who receives it."*

In John 6:48-63 Jesus makes it clear that He is the true manna that was sent from heaven. Unlike the manna that the Children of Israel received from God to sustain their physical bodies during their journey through the wilderness, Jesus is the spiritual food and drink that every person needs in order to gain eternal life. For the words He speaks are life to all mankind, if they choose to follow them. Every individual who enters into a personal relationship with Jesus will receive the hidden manna; for it is a precious bond between you and the Saviour which no-one can interrupt, or break down.

For the significance of the white stone, we must look to the gladiators of old. Victorious gladiators in Greece and Rome were given white stones engraved with their names, which they could use to gain privileges. Jesus promises that as victors we will receive the white stone of victory, inscribed with our new name; a name that reveals how we have overcome. In the Bible, it was common for people, who had finally given themselves wholeheartedly to God, to receive a name change; such as Abraham, Sarah, Jacob and Paul. Likewise, our new name will be indicative of our journey from a sinful life to salvation in Jesus.

The message to the church in Thyatira

Revelation 2:18 – Jesus instructs John to write to the leader of the church situated in Thyatira. He identifies Himself as *". . . Son of God"* who has eyes like blazing fire and feet like burnished bronze. Once again this follows the description of Jesus in Revelation 1:14,15 which confirms His divinity.

Revelation 2:19 – Jesus knows the state of His church, both at the time John was writing, and through the Thyatiran era (AD538 – 1798). This period in history is known as the Dark Ages, and is also referred to in the Book of Daniel as the time of great persecution of God's people by the Roman Catholic Church (see Daniel 7:25). This time of cruel oppression will come up again in Revelation chapters eleven, twelve and thirteen. It is therefore a significant period for God's church.

Jesus commends the Thyatira church for its deeds, love, faith, service, perseverance, and, that its work has improved.

Revelation 2:20 – However, Jesus is not completely satisfied with the church for it tolerates *". . . that woman Jezebel"*. Jezebel was the infamous queen married to king Ahab (a weak king of Israel in Old Testament times). Jezebel killed God's prophets, led the Jewish nation into worshiping the heathen idol god, Baal, and threatened the life of Elijah, God's prophet (see 1 Kings 16:29 – 1 Kings 19:18). Jesus warns that Jezebel calls herself a prophet, but her teachings mislead God's people into sexual immorality and the eating of food sacrificed to idols. And, in ancient times, this is exactly what happened; the worship of Baal involved promiscuity on a massive scale, and the people's food was offered up to the idol.

While Jesus' reference to Jezebel, and her teachings, serve as a literal warning of behaviour to be avoided by the Thyatiran church of John's time, we can also look for a symbolic application.

Here, we are introduced to another prophetic rule, namely that women in prophecy symbolise churches. In Ezekiel 16 we see God dealing with His people as a suitor courting a woman who goes astray. Jeremiah 6:2 refers to Zion (God's people) as a daughter, beautiful and delicate. And, in Ephesians

5:25-27, Christ's church is described as His wife. We will become more familiar with this symbol throughout Revelation where a virtuous woman represents God's true church, and an impure woman represents an apostate church.

It seems clear, the sexual immorality and idol worship taught by this symbolic Jezebel refers to the adoption of all false doctrine that leads to the church being unfaithful to Christ. We will see the theme of spiritual immorality repeated throughout Revelation. God seeks a pure church; one that remains true to Him.

Revelation 2:21 – Jesus points out He has been merciful and given the apostates within His church ample time to repent, but they have refused. Therefore, action must now be taken.

Revelation 2:22 – Jesus warns, He will cast Jezebel on a bed of suffering, and those who commit adultery with her will also suffer intensely, unless they repent. During the Thyatiran era (AD538-1798) God's church was massively altered by the doctrines of the Roman Catholic Church. The Church of Rome called itself Christian but brought into its worship, practices that denied the role and ministry of Jesus, such as Mass with its teaching of transubstantiation (the host (bread) and wine are changed into the actual body and blood of Christ). The Mass is, therefore, an attempt to recreate the death of Christ over and over again, whereas the Bible teaches Jesus' death for our sins was a once-for-all event (see Hebrews 10:10).

The Catholic Church also continued the use of altars and incense in its worship, which were part of the Jewish sacrificial system done away with by Jesus' death. In addition, this church introduced other un-Biblical practices such as the confessing of sins to priests; the selling of indulgences that allowed the praying of souls out of Purgatory (a place of purification for dead souls, also invented by the Catholic Church); the worship of Mary and the Apostles; the conferring of sainthood; and many more. These teachings, instituted by the Church of Rome, were forced upon Christian worshipers, who were martyred if they refused to adhere. Jesus promises that people who participate in spiritual adultery with this false church will *"suffer intensely"* unless they repent. As the true church is the faithful wife of Jesus, any individual who follows after, and unites with, an apostate church is committing spiritual adultery.

Revelation 2:23 – Jesus also promises that Jezebel's children will be struck dead. As Jezebel symbolises the apostate Church of Rome, then all churches that adopt her teachings must be her children, including Protestant churches following her lead. Indeed, the Catholic Church today refers to itself as the Mother of Christendom, and to Protestant churches as its wayward children.

Jesus then confirms that He is actually speaking about churches here. He says *"Then all the churches will know that I am he who searches hearts and minds. . ."* He who has eyes like blazing fire sees into the hearts of professed Christians. He discerns whether they are true to Him or, in reality, committing spiritual adultery. He then repays each person for their deeds. In other words, He is a God of justice. Each person will receive their just deserts.

Revelation 2:24-25 – But, not all in His church will follow apostate doctrines. Some will not tolerate false teachings. Jesus describes these as, those who have *"not learned Satan's so-called deep secrets . . ."* Could it be that the Roman Catholic Church teaches doctrines that come from the devil himself?

(Please see this quotation from 'The Seven Epistles of Christ' - Taylor G Bunch page 172.)

"The Catholics boast of having adopted and Christianised paganism in order to defeat Satan with his own religion. Thus paganism with its mysteries and the deep things of Satan became the religion of the church during the Thyatiran period."

Jesus says, those who have rejected the teachings of the apostate church will not be subjected to any additional burden. They are encouraged to hold on to the truth they already know, until He comes.

Revelation 2:26-27 – Jesus promises that, just as He has been given authority by His Father, those who do His will to the end will gain authority over nations, rule them with an iron sceptre and dash them to pieces like pottery. This indicates that His people, presently suffering dire persecution from the powerful rulers of their time, will see the tables turn at the end of time. They will be given a role in meting out punishment to their persecutors. They will be given the authority they lacked in their earthly lives, to carry out the Lord's judgement.

Revelation 2:28 – Jesus also promises to give His victorious one the "*morning star*". Some suggest the '*morning star*' refers to the great Protestant Reformation that rejected the false teachings of the Church of Rome. An early English Reformer was John Wycliffe, who in the 1300s translated the Bible from Latin to English. Wycliffe led the way for other protestors such as Martin Luther (1483 – 1546), and many others. It is said the Protestant Reformers dispelled the darkness of Papal apostasy, and therefore could well be described as the 'morning star' that would lead the way for the great enlightenment to come. Revelation 22:16 refers to Jesus as "*the bright Morning Star*", a reminder that He is the "*...light of the world*" (John 9:5) who brings the truth of salvation to humanity. Therefore, the "*morning star*" of Revelation 2:28 must certainly be related to the truth of Jesus Christ, and could indeed be the Protestant uprising that brought truth to light in a time of spiritual darkness.

Revelation 2:29 - Jesus concludes the message to the Thyatira church with the now familiar phrase "*Whoever has ears, let them hear what the Spirit says to the churches.*" This message is important; pay attention.

Revelation Chapter Three

SARDIS, PHILADELPHIA AND LAODICEA

Based on Revelation 3:1-22

The messages to the seven churches continue. In Revelation chapter three we see the final three churches addressed.

The message to the church in Sardis

Revelation 3:1 – Jesus instructs John to write to the leader of the church in Sardis a specific message for the church. He identifies Himself as the one *who ". . . holds the seven spirits of God and the seven stars."* We know from Revelation 1:4 the "seven spirits of God" is none other than the third person of the Godhead, the Holy Spirit. The seven stars are identified in Revelation 1:20 as the leaders of the seven churches. Therefore, we are reminded that Jesus is the Head of the true church throughout history: He holds its leaders in His hands and directs them through the working of the Holy Spirit. An encouraging start. However, Jesus has no commendation for this particular church. He says, *"I know your deeds"*. Although the church of Sardis is undoubtedly His church, it has a false reputation, for it purports to be alive when it is actually dead.

The Sardis historical era (1798-1833) followed the great Protestant Reformation during which brave Reformers, like Martin Luther, broke away from the Roman Catholic Church with its erroneous doctrines. Luther, especially, brought to light the Biblical doctrine pivotal to Christianity; righteousness by faith alone, which totally discredited the Catholic dictate that God requires the performance of penances to gain Divine favour. However, despite the great work of the Reformers, the church of the Sardis era failed to uphold the pure Protestant faith. Although it called itself Protestant, its continued adherence to many Roman Catholic practices, earned its designation of being spiritually dead.

Revelation 3:2-3 – Jesus gives the church of Sardis the solution to its condition. It is not too late; it can wake up. There are parts of the church still alive. Jesus says, "*Strengthen what is alive and is about to die.*" He instructs the church to remember the true doctrine it first believed; to hold on to it and repent its adoption of error. But, He also warns that if the church refuses to awake, He will come "*like a thief*" and it will not know He has come.

It is interesting that Jesus speaks of His coming when Sardis is not the final church (there are two more churches to come). What could Jesus be referring to when he warns, "*I will come like a thief*"? As we shall see, this is best explained by the next church era, Philadelphia; the time of great spiritual awakening. Jesus is warning that if the church of the Sardis era remains in its spiritual lethargy it will miss out on the spiritual revival soon to come.

Revelation 3:4-5 - There is good news for the Sardis church. It contains a faithful few who have kept themselves spiritually pure. Jesus describes them as having "*not soiled their clothes*". The doctrine of righteousness by faith, highlighted by Martin Luther, alerts every believer to their need to be covered with Christ's robe of righteousness. Only in this way can they be viewed by God the Father as fitted for His kingdom (see Isaiah 61:10). The robe is pure and white. It bears no stain of sin. It shows our victory over wrong-doing through the blood of the Lamb, Jesus Christ. We obtain this symbolic robe by confessing our sins to God, and admitting that we are incapable of being good in, or of, ourselves. Then our faith lays hold on the promise that because Jesus died in our place, our acceptance of His sacrifice allows God to treat us as if we had never sinned. This is the robe of righteousness that covers us and allows us into the kingdom of God. Jesus promises that everyone dressed in this robe will have their names written in the Book of Life, and He will acknowledge them before God the Father and the holy angels. (We will come across the Book of Life again in Revelation.)

Revelation 3:6 – Once again, Jesus repeats the phrase *"Whoever has ears, let them hear what the Spirit says to the churches."* He seeks our full attention: the message to the church in Sardis is for everyone. We need to wake up from spiritual sleep and hold on to the truth. We need to realise we are sinners, confess our sins to God, and by faith accept the righteousness of Jesus. Moreover, we must keep that robe spotless by living a life guided and powered by the Holy Spirit. Only then, can our names be retained in the Book of Life, which designates us as heirs of eternal life. No wonder Jesus warns us to listen carefully: He is giving us the formula for our own salvation.

The message to the church in Philadelphia

Revelation 3:7 – Jesus gives John the message he is to write to the leader of the church situated in Philadelphia, Asia. He describes Himself as *"holy and true"* and the one *"who holds the key of David"*. Jesus is God and so of course is holy. We are called to be holy as God is holy (see 1 Peter 1:16). And, He is the God of truth (see Isaiah 65:16 [KJV]). Therefore, we are once again assured that this message comes from God, and we can trust His word.

The 'key of David' is an interesting term. Both the key and the door it opens are significant. Only Jesus is qualified to use the key, and only He can open the door. When He opens this door, it remains open, and when He closes it, it remains closed.

But why is the key specifically the 'key of David'? Jesus is described as the Messiah, and son of David (see Matthew 1:1) because His human genealogy came through the line of king David. David was not a perfect man. He committed terrible sins. Yet his continued relationship with God confirms that he knew God to be a merciful and forgiving God; one who will always accept us if we repent of our sins (see Psalm 51). David was a valiant soldier for the Lord, who, as a boy, felt able to run at Goliath with just a sling and a stone, because he believed the Lord was with Him (see 1 Samuel 17:1-54). David continually put his trust in God and not in human beings (see 2 Samuel 24:14). David was the earthly king of ancient Jerusalem. Jesus is the heavenly King of the New Jerusalem. Thus, the key of David signifies:

- Jesus, the Messiah
- Jesus, the heir of a royal genealogy
- Jesus, the merciful and forgiving God
- Jesus, the God who fights for his children
- Jesus, the God who can be trusted
- Jesus, the King of heaven

This key in the hand of Jesus opens the door of salvation and no-one else can close it. Those who choose Jesus will be saved, no-one can prevent them. Those who reject Jesus as Saviour cannot be saved. Salvation is closed to them, and whatever Jesus closes, no-one else can open. As Acts 4:12 says *"for there is no other name under heaven given to mankind by which we must be saved."*

Revelation 3:8 – Jesus assures the Philadelphia church that He is well acquainted with its deeds. It only has a little strength, but it is a faithful church; one that has kept His word and not denied His name.

The ancient Philadelphia church was small but faithful to the teachings of Jesus. Likewise, God's church during the Philadelphian historical period (1833-1844) was a small gathering that stuck close to the faith of Jesus. This era is known as the great spiritual awakening. It began small, and with little strength.

Involved in the awakening were Americans like William Miller, Josiah Litch and Joshua Himes, English men like Robert Winter, the widely travelled German, Dr Joseph Wolff, and others. These Christian men began to study the Bible with new fervour, and subsequently preach that the coming of Jesus was near.

Their Bible study was centred on the prophecies of Daniel, specifically Daniel chapters 8 and 9 which highlighted a seemingly new and little known prophecy - The 2,300 days. This prophecy tells of the cleansing of the sanctuary, which in Leviticus 16 is called the Day of Atonement.

The aim of the annual Day of Atonement was to rid the Jewish sanctuary of the sins of God's people. It was the one time in the year when the High Priest entered the Most Holy Place of the sanctuary, bearing the blood of the slain goat sacrifice, there to plead the cleansing of the confessed sins of the people before the Mercy Seat. Only then could these sins be transferred to the rightful animal, the scapegoat, and so the sanctuary was cleansed (see Leviticus 16). The 19th century Bible scholars now saw that this earthly ceremony pointed towards a heavenly event affecting Jews and Gentiles alike.

Here is what their Bible study revealed about the cleansing of the sanctuary situated in heaven:

The life deeds of God's professed people are recorded in the books of heaven. At the appointed time, the investigation of these books would begin. This investigation was prophesied to commence at the end of the prophetic 2,300 days. The examination of the books would take the form of a judgement of all those professing to believe in Jesus, to see whether they had truly confessed their sins, given their lives to Jesus, and were thus covered by His atoning blood. This judgement, described in Daniel 7:9-10, 13-14, the scholars named 'The Investigative Judgement', because it involved the investigation of the lives of God's people. It is the judgement that takes place before Jesus comes back to earth to rescue His people, and it began on 22 October 1844. (For a full explanation of the 2,300 Day prophecy, please see the companion to this book 'An Idiot's Guide to the Book of Daniel' Chapters 7-9).

Now, the promise of Jesus in Revelation 3:7,8:

". . .What He opens no-one can shut, and what He shuts no-one can open . . . See, I have placed before you an open door that no one can shut. . ."

This promise took on special meaning for the little flock of the Philadelphian era. They understood the open door to be more than the door of salvation: it was the door in the heavenly sanctuary that led to the Most Holy Place where Jesus was now pleading His blood for them before His Father in the Investigative Judgement. In order to open this door Jesus had shut the door of the Holy Place (the first compartment of the temple) where He had been ministering since His ascension. Jesus' ministration in the second compartment began in 1844, and would be the last phase of His heavenly ministry before coming back to earth. The Philadelphia brethren rejoiced that no-one would be able to stop this work performed by Jesus on their behalf.

(In Revelation 10 we will examine in detail the story of the Philadelphian believers.)

Revelation 3:9 – This small group of true believers was fiercely derided by the mainstream Christian churches of the day. However, Jesus identifies those who oppose His church of the Philadelphian period as the *"synagogue of Satan, who claim to be Jews though they are not"*. He further states they are liars who will be forced to fall down at the feet of God's people and acknowledge them as beloved by God.

Revelation 3:10 – Jesus goes on to promise that the patient endurance of His church will be rewarded. It will be kept from the trials earth's inhabitants will experience. In Revelation chapters 15 and 16 we will see the great trials that will come on the world: they are called the Seven Last Plagues. Jesus promises His people will not suffer these terrible judgements to come.

Another interpretation of this promise is that the Philadelphian brethren would be kept from the trials because they would not be alive when the last plagues are unleashed. In His mercy God would lay them to sleep so they would not have to go through this troubled time. As the Bible scholars of the Philadelphian era studied the prophetic book of Daniel, they realised the time of the end began in 1798; and over 200 years later we are still in the last period of earth's history. Truly, Jesus can come at any time, but as the Bible says, it will seem as if He is delaying His coming (see 2 Peter 3:3-13). The Philadelphian brethren were informed that although they were now in the time of the end, they would not live to see the fearful final events that would usher in Jesus' coming.

Daniel chapter seven's description of the Investigative Judgement shows that as soon as the final verdict is given, Jesus returns to the earth for His people.

Revelation 3:11- Jesus states *"I am coming soon"*. There is no delay in His coming, but as 2 Peter 3:3-13 states; God is merciful. He waits patiently for men to make a decision to follow Him, but we must be careful not to allow ourselves to be lulled into a false sense of security. Jesus will come at the appointed time and those who scoff because He has not already come, will be taken unawares.

There is no criticism of the Philadelphian church, they are only admonished to hold on to the truth they have. They must not give up so near to the end. They must not let anyone take away their heavenly crowns.

Revelation 3:12 – Jesus outlines the reward awaiting the Philadelphian brethren who hold on to the truth. They will become pillars in the temple of God; permanent fixtures in the heavenly temple. Jesus has opened the way into the heavenly temple's Most Holy Place and now He promises they will never leave. Their right to inhabit the temple situated in the New Jerusalem (the city of God) is signified by the fact that they will bear three new names:

- The name of God the Father
- The name of the New Jerusalem
- Jesus' new name

No-one will again be able to question their citizenship in the kingdom of God.

Revelation 3:13 – Here is the usual instruction from Jesus "*Whoever has ears, let them hear what the Spirit says to the churches.*" This message is important: you need to listen and understand its significance for you. We all need to hear the message to the Philadelphian church, for God has opened the way into the Most Holy Place for us all. We need to confess our sins to Him, and trust in the shed blood of Jesus, so that when the book of our deeds is opened in the Investigative Judgement, it will be seen that Jesus has covered us with His righteousness. We must be aware that we are now in the time of the end, and as soon as the last verdict is pronounced by our heavenly Father, Jesus will come quickly to gather His people from the earth, for this planet is earmarked for destruction. We need to hold on to this truth and reserve our place in heaven.

The message to the church in Laodicea

Revelation 3:14 – John is instructed to write to the leader of the church situated in Laodicea. This is the seventh and last letter to the churches.

The word Laodicea means 'a people judged' or 'the judgement of the people'. This period is clearly the time of the Investigative Judgement. It began in 1844, continues today, and will end just before Jesus comes. Therefore, as we are now living in the Laodicean period, this message is specifically for us.

Jesus identifies Himself: He is the "*Amen* (let it be so); *the faithful and true witness; the ruler of God's creation*". Once again, Jesus uses one of His descriptions from Revelation 1 (verse 5). He is confirming that we can trust the source of this message: He is not only faithful; He is the ruler of God's creation; therefore, He is God.

Revelation 3:15-16 – Jesus knows His end time church. Its members are neither cold nor hot. As a result, they are neither fully committed to Him, nor have they fully rejected Him. They are somewhere in the middle; lukewarm or lack lustre; one foot in the church, the other in the world. They say they are followers of Christ but they show no enthusiasm or vigour. Jesus says, He wishes they were either cold or hot. If they were hot, they would truly be His children. If they were cold, they might realise their need of Him, and give their hearts to Him, but because they are lukewarm, they see no need of change. They are gently simmering; a mixture of hot and cold.

The lukewarm condition is distasteful to Jesus: it makes Him sick. A hot drink warms the body, a cold drink refreshes, but a lukewarm drink is insipid. Jesus says, *"I am about to spit you out of my mouth."* Ancient Laodicea was well known for its lukewarm springs, that when drunk caused nausea. Hence, the city is a fitting example of the state of God's church.

Revelation 3:17 – The truth is, lukewarm Christians do not feel in need. They are comfortable. They know the truth and follow it to a certain degree. They feel satisfied, and are self-satisfied. They say *"I am rich; I have acquired wealth and do not need a thing."* But they are unaware of their true condition. Actually, Jesus identifies them as *"wretched, pitiful, poor, blind and naked"*, and they don't realise it. What a terrible condition to be in.

The Apostles were on fire for the Lord and spread the gospel with joy and urgency. The Gentiles at the time were cold to the gospel of Jesus Christ, but when they heard the message of Christ crucified they accepted the good news with glad hearts and embraced the truth. But, instead of taking up its responsibility to preach the gospel to the world, the end time church is resting on its laurels, believing its knowledge of the truth will secure its place in heaven. How unfortunate, that although God's people, living in the last days of earth's history, are aware the Investigative Judgement is taking place in heaven, and Jesus is soon to come, they are not aroused from their lethargy.

Revelation 3:18 - Jesus gives no commendation to the Laodicean church, but theirs is not a hopeless case. He gives the remedy for the church's condition.

If they are to wake from their lukewarm state, the Laodicean brethren must buy three items from Him, namely:

- Gold refined in the fire (so they can become rich);
- White clothes (so they can cover their shameful nakedness);
- Eye salve (so they can see).

As Jesus is speaking of His people's spiritual lack, we can safely assume the above items are symbolic of spiritual necessities.

1 Peter 1:7-9 tell us that our **faith in Jesus**, that leads us to **love** Him and follow Him, is like gold refined in fire.

Isaiah 61:10 tells us that Jesus covers us with **garments of salvation and a robe of righteousness.**

John 16:8-10, 13-15 tell us, it is the **Holy Spirit** who reveals to us our true spiritual condition, and opens our eyes to the truth from God.

The three items are identified:

- **faith that leads to loving service** and makes us rich towards God;
- the saving, **righteous character of Jesus** that covers our unrighteous, spiritually naked bodies;
- **the Holy Spirit** who enables us to discern our true spiritual condition.

These items are only available from Jesus. We are instructed to buy them from Him. But what currency could we give for these priceless items? The currency is our hearts (see Ezekiel 36:26,27). When we give our hearts to Jesus, that is, commit ourselves to Him, then He develops in us a faith that leads us to love and serve Him. He covers us with His own righteousness that fits us for heaven and eternal life. And, He sends the Comforter, the Holy Spirit, to open our spiritual eyesight to see our constant need of the character of Jesus. Then, day-by-day as we continue to surrender our hearts, the Holy Spirit changes us, and we become like Jesus. This is the remedy for the Laodicean condition.

Revelation 3:19-20 – Jesus says *"Those whom I love, I rebuke and discipline. So be earnest and repent. Here I stand at the door and knock. If anyone hears my voice and opens the door, I will come in and eat with that person, and they with me."*

What wonderful words of love and encouragement. Jesus is surely speaking to the individual here. He is not angry at our lukewarm state. He loves us, and wants to save us. Just as with a child who needs to be corrected, He advises His wayward children to turn around and seek a change. He will not force any of us to be saved. He waits, patiently knocking at our hearts' door. We have to open the door and let Him in so He can clean us up and make us fit for heaven. This is likened to enjoying a delicious meal with our Saviour. It is a life of loving communication, and enlightenment, as we become acquainted with the Redeemer of humankind. This relationship leads nowhere else but to eternal life.

Revelation 3:21 – Here is the reward for those who allow Jesus into their hearts; a right to sit on Jesus' throne with Him. When Jesus overcame sin and death on earth, and ascended to heaven, He was allowed to sit with God the Father on His throne. We get the same treatment. What will we have done to deserve such honour? Nothing. Nothing at all. That is the nature of God. He gives us the very thing we do not deserve. What grace! What love! Truly, it is too much to comprehend.

Revelation 3:22 – Finally, Jesus says to the last of the seven churches *"Whoever has ears, let them hear what the Spirit says to the churches."* This is the most important information ever given to mankind. We need to listen.

Revelation Chapter Four

GOD'S THRONE ROOM

Based on Revelation 4:1-11

As with chapter one, Revelation 4 is an introduction: a new vision is about to be revealed.

Revelation 4:1 – John sees an open door in heaven, and a voice that sounds like a trumpet invites him to come and see things that are going to happen. John heard the trumpet-like voice of Jesus in Revelation 1:10, now the same voice is addressing him in chapter four, an indication this vision comes from the same Divine source.

Revelation 4:2 – Just as in chapter one, John is transported in vision by the Holy Spirit. This time he is taken through the open door into the heavenly throne room of God the Father. He sees the throne and then someone comes to sit on it. The Old Testament prophet, Ezekiel, was also shown a vision of God's throne room. He describes the throne as being made of *"lapis Lazuli"* (Ezekiel 1:25). We know lapis Lazuli to be a much sought after blue crystal gem stone – the universal symbol of wisdom and truth. (www.crystalvaults.com/crystal-encyclopedia/lapislazuli) Thus, even the heavenly throne testifies of the character of God.

Revelation 4:3 – John describes the person seated on the throne as having the appearance of jasper and ruby. How do you describe God? John did his best. Yet, it is difficult to imagine a person glowing like multiple gem stones. (Jasper has within it the colours of red, yellow, brown, green and even blue. Rubies range from pink to blood red).

While God sparkles like precious stones, a shimmering emerald rainbow encircles His throne. The rainbow reminds us that God is a person who keeps covenants with His people. The first rainbow, He placed in the clouds as a covenant with all creatures on the earth; giving the assurance He would never again destroy the earth by a flood (see Genesis 9:12-17). Throughout the Bible, we see God making covenants with His people; promises to save them; to protect them; to deliver them. No wonder there is a covenant symbol encircling His throne: He is a faithful covenant-keeping God. The rainbow reminds us that God makes promises to His children, and He fulfils them.

Revelation 4:4 – And, in the throne room John sees people. They are not angels. They are described as 'elders' and there are twenty-four of them seated on thrones that surround the throne of God. They are dressed in white and wear golden crowns. Are they deity too? We are given clues to their identity. Firstly, they are called elders. They do not shine like precious gems, as God does. Acts 15:4 describes the leaders of the church as *"elders"*. An elder is a human being; a leader in the church. Secondly, they are seated on thrones. Revelation 3:21 tells us those redeemed from the earth will sit on thrones in heaven. Thirdly, the twenty-four elders are wearing white robes. Revelation 7:9 describes the saved people of earth as wearing white robes and standing before the throne of God. Fourthly, the elders wear golden crowns. 2 Timothy 4:7,8 tell us, all those who have kept the faith are destined to receive a crown of righteousness. All these clues help build a picture of the identity of the twenty-four elders. They appear to be humans who have been faithful to God, and are now in heaven around His throne. But how can they already be in heaven when the Bible tells us all those who inherit eternal life (whether they have died or are still alive) will travel to heaven together when Jesus comes back to earth? Indeed, the reason for His coming is to collect His faithful people, both the living and the dead (see 1 Thessalonians 4:13-18).

There is an interesting account in Matthew 27:50-53 of miraculous events at the time of Jesus' death. The Jerusalem temple curtain was torn in two from top to bottom, exposing the Most Holy Place, which was forbidden to anyone other than the High Priest; thus signifying the end of the Jewish ceremonial worship system. At the same time, there was a terrible earthquake which caused rocks to split, tombs to open, and many of the dead came to life. After Jesus rose from the dead, this resurrected group entered Jerusalem and appeared to people there. We do not hear anything more of them, for example, there is no record of them helping to spread the gospel with the apostles in the book of Acts. However, we are told that when Jesus ascended to heaven, He took with Him many 'captives' (see Ephesians 4:8). Could it be that the twenty-four elders are those resurrected at Jesus' death? They were captives of death, liberated by Jesus, and now we see them seated around the throne of God in heaven.

Why twenty-four elders? In 1 Chronicles 24:7-19 we find twenty-four Levite men from the families of the priests, appointed to serve in the temple of the Lord. It is therefore interesting that there are also twenty-four elders serving God in the heavenly throne room. We already know from Hebrews 8 that the earthly sanctuary was a copy of the temple in heaven. Thus, we may conclude that the 24 people resurrected at Jesus' death are not a random number. They were specifically raised to officiate in heaven, and are (with Christ) the firstfruits of the resurrection of the redeemed; guaranteeing the resurrection of the righteous at Jesus' second coming (see 1 Corinthians 15:20-23). As, in the earthly sanctuary, the twenty-four elders officiated in the Holy Place (or first compartment), we can conclude that the throne room in heaven, where the resurrected twenty-four elders officiate, is the Holy Place (first compartment) of the heavenly temple.

Revelation 4:5 – God's throne room is not a place of silence: there are flashes of lightning and peals of thunder. Ezekiel 1:14 and 10:5 tell us the angels in heaven cause flashes of lightning when they move, and the sound of their wings is like the voice of God Almighty which thunders (see Psalm 29:3). It appears that within the throne room angels fly at speed causing lightning and thunder. In front of God's throne are seven blazing lamps representing the seven spirits of God, which we already know, from Revelation 1, signify the presence of the Holy Spirit.

We have also learned that the seven lamps are present in the Holy Place of the heavenly temple. Further proof that God the Father is seated on His throne in the first compartment of the temple.

Revelation 4:6-8 – In front of God's throne is a surface that looks like a sea of glass as *"clear as crystal"*. Ezekiel describes this as an awesome expanse sparkling like crystal (Ezekiel 1:22). Then, John describes a group of angelic beings, whom he calls the *"four living creatures"*. These angels also appeared in visions of the prophet Ezekiel (see Ezekiel 1 and 10). Ezekiel calls them Cherubim. If we combine the descriptions of John and Ezekiel, we get a complete picture of these extraordinary beings.

The Four Cherubim:

- They are humanoid in appearance but each has four faces (human in front, lion on the right side, ox on the left side, eagle at the back);
- John says they have six wings (Ezekiel sees only four wings). The sound of their flapping wings is like thunder;
- They have straight legs with calf's feet that glow like burnished bronze;
- They have human hands;
- Their bodies appear to be filled with fire, and fire moves back and forth between them;
- They are covered with eyes because they look to and fro throughout the earth;
- Ezekiel describes how they stand in a line with their wings touching, and move in unison;
- They speed back and forth causing lightning flashes as they move;
- They are in the throne room of God;

- Ezekiel describes them as directing the wheels of God's throne: God's throne is mobile (see Daniel 7:9).

These are strange beings indeed, but their form is also significant and symbolic. (See the following quotation from 'www.revelationbibleprophecy.org/revelation4'):

"The four different faces upon these living creatures also represent to us something about Christ. With Israel in the wilderness, the twelve tribes were divided into four groups around the tabernacle of God. Each of these groups went by a standard or symbol. Judah was the lion, Reuben was the man, Ephraim the ox or calf, and Dan the eagle. Just as the living creatures, with these characteristics, are about the throne where God dwells; so too are the tribes of Israel, with these symbols, encamped around the sanctuary where God was dwelling (Exodus 25:8). The lion stands for the kingship or rulership of Christ, the man the humanity of Christ and His priestly role, the ox the service and sacrifice of Christ, and the eagle the divinity of Christ. Notice too that the lion is the king of the beasts, the ox is the head of the cattle, man is the head of humanity, and the eagle is head of the birds. This is quite clearly pointing to the coming Messiah."

The Cherubim have a role in heaven's temple, they never stop saying:

" Holy, holy, holy
is the Lord God Almighty,
Who was, and is, and is to come."

They constantly praise God. Is this because they are compelled to worship? No, they speak only what is true. They know who God is; they are in His presence day and night; they know He is holy, that He is truly the Almighty God, and that He has always existed, exists now, and will always exist. Why not proclaim it?

Revelation 4:9-11 – As soon as the Cherubim begin to praise God, the twenty-four elders join in. They fall down in front of God and lay their golden crowns before Him. They say:

"You are worthy, our Lord and God,
to receive glory and honour and power,
for you created all things,
and by your will they were created
and have their being."

Why do we on planet earth fail to worship God in this way? He is indeed the Creator of all things. We would not exist without Him, and yet the vast majority of earth's inhabitants do not even acknowledge Him. Those who live in His presence naturally fall down to worship Him. They know He deserves our honour and adoration. They delight in giving glory to the self-existent one.

John's vision of the heavenly throne room shows a place of wonder, majesty, magnificent heavenly beings, rolling thunder and flashing lightning, a shimmering rainbow, the constant sound of praise and worship, and in the midst of it all is God, glittering and glowing like precious jewels, the Creator of the universe seated on His throne.

The scene has been set: something important is about to happen.

Revelation Chapter Five

THE SCROLL OPENER

Based on Revelation 5:1-14

Revelation chapter five continues to set the scene for the next message John will be given. This new message given in Revelation 6-8 is so important, the stage must be set. Revelation 4 shows us into the throne room of God in heaven; the first compartment of the heavenly temple (The Holy Place). This is where the message comes from. Chapter five tells us who the message is from. We have witnessed this scene setting before in Revelation chapter one. Before the message is given, it is important for us to know its orientation, and its originator.

There are those who read the book of Revelation picking and choosing which parts to believe, but from the beginning of the book (Revelation 1:1-3), throughout the book (Revelation 4 and 5), and at the book's conclusion (Revelation 22:18,19), God makes it clear that the entire book is Divine in origin.

Revelation 4 shows God the Father taking His seat on the throne.

Revelation 5:1 – Now that He is seated, John notices He is holding a scroll in His right hand. Why His right hand? Psalms 20:6 and 18:35 tell us God's right hand represents *"saving"* and *"sustaining strength"*. Therefore, right at the beginning of chapter five, God is declaring Himself as our Saviour and Sustainer: He has good intentions for us.

The scroll in God's hand has writing on both sides. As we are never told what is actually written in the scroll, we can put forward some informed suggestions.

Here is one suggestion taken from www.revelationbibleprophecy.org/revelation5:

The practice of writing on both the inside and outside of a scroll in Bible times was reserved for the writing of title deeds for redeeming a lost inheritance. If a land owner fell on hard times and had to sell his land due to poverty, a near relative, or kinsman, could purchase (or redeem) the land from the buyer, in order to return it to his relative. In this way, the family inheritance could be retained. The deeds for the redeeming of land were written on the inside of the scroll. Then the witness statements and signatures attesting to the transaction were written on the outside. Thus, the scroll of Revelation 5 reminds us of the plan of salvation. As shown in the quotation below from 'An Exposition of Revelation 5' - An Enduring Vision (Revelation Revealed) - page 13.

"Adam and Eve were established in Eden by the Creator. Through disobedience they sold out their inheritance to Satan and went out to the land of the enemy, the land of death. But a remnant of Adam's family has sought to return to Eden and regain the lost inheritance. They have found a new kinsman – one of their own race – through whom the inheritance can be redeemed and restored. Jesus Christ has paid the debt of Adam's race upon Calvary's cross. By the sacrifice of His life, He has redeemed the lost inheritance."

Alternatively, the reason that writing is on both the inside and outside of the scroll may simply be because the scroll contains so much information.

The scroll in God's hand is sealed with seven seals. A normal scroll has one seal but this scroll is special. We have already seen in Revelation chapter one the significance of the number seven. The Seven Seals designate the scroll as spiritually perfect and complete; and why wouldn't it be, it originated from God Himself.

Revelation 5:2 – A mighty angel appears asking in a loud voice *"Who is worthy to break the seals and open the scroll?"* Obviously, it takes a special person to open a special scroll: someone with the right authority, and appropriate qualifications.

Revelation 5:3 – Sadly, no-one can be found in heaven, earth or under the earth, eligible to open the Seven Seals, or read the scroll. No angels, not even God the Father, nor God the Holy Spirit. No-one now living, and no-one now dead and buried, can take on this task. How can it be that neither God the Father nor the Holy Spirit, who both have all authority and power, are eligible to open the scroll? As we will find out, not even they have the necessary qualifications for the job.

Revelation 5:4-5 – John begins to cry because it seems the scroll will never be opened. However, he is comforted by one of the twenty-four elders who tells him the Lion of the Tribe of Judah, also called the Root of David, is able to open the Seven Seals. Who is this person? Genesis 49:8-10 introduces the tribe of Judah as a lion, and the Messianic prophecy identifies exactly who that lion is *"The sceptre will not depart from Judah, nor the ruler's staff from between his feet, until he to whom it belongs shall come and the obedience of the nations shall be his."* Jesus was born into the tribe of Judah, just as predicted. Matthew 21:9 tells us that on Palm Sunday the crowds hailed Him as the *"Son of David"* a name identifying the Messiah. Moreover, in Matthew 22:41-45 Jesus identifies Himself as both 'Son of David' and 'Son of God'. Thus, He is the Son of David, because as a man he came through David's line, but, He is also God; David's Creator, and therefore the Root of David.

Revelation 5:6 – Then Jesus, the Lion of the Tribe of Judah appears, not as a lion but as a Lamb with its throat cut. Jesus is God, but He chose to come to earth and become the Lamb that was slain (see Isaiah 53, Hebrews 9:13-14, John 1:29). For the task of opening the scroll Jesus chooses to present Himself as the Sacrificial Offering and Saviour of humanity. He stands front and centre before the throne of God. Whatever is contained within the scroll, Jesus, the one who died for our sins, will open it for us.

The twenty-four elders and the four Cherubim encircle the Lamb and John now sees the lamb has seven horns and seven eyes – The New Living Translation Bible describes it this way *"He had seven horns and seven eyes, which represent the sevenfold Spirit of God that is sent out into every part of the earth."* Revelation chapter one identifies the Seven-fold Spirit as the perfect Holy Spirit. Jesus and the Holy Spirit are inextricably bound together. When He was on earth, Jesus let us know that once He had ascended, God the Father would send the Holy Spirit to go throughout the earth to comfort us in Jesus' absence, remind us of Him and make us like Him (see John 14:26, John 15:26, John 16:13,14). Consequently, the image of Jesus, now seen in the heavenly throne room by John, is our Saviour who carries in His person the representation of the Holy Spirit, whose job it is to unfold the character of Jesus throughout the earth.

Revelation 5:7 - The Lamb takes the scroll from the right hand of God the Father.

Revelation 5:8 - The twenty-four elders and the Cherubim are so overjoyed that the scroll opener has been found, they fall down and worship the Lamb. Each elder holds both a harp and a golden bowl of incense. We are told the incense represents the prayers of God's people. It appears the role of the elders in the heavenly temple is to present to God the prayers of His righteous ones – much as the Levite Priests did in the wilderness sanctuary (see Psalm 141:2, Exodus 30:7,8). We should never be tempted to think that God pays no attention to our prayers. The twenty-four elders hold our petitions in front of God at all times: He cannot forget or ignore them. They are ever before Him.

Revelation 5:9-10 - The fact that Jesus chooses to represent Himself as the Saviour of mankind is not lost on the twenty-four elders who use their harps to sing a new song. This is the song of celebration (New King James Version):

"You are worthy to take the scroll,
and to open its seals;
for You were slain,
and have redeemed us to God by Your blood
out of every tribe and tongue and people and nation,
and have made us kings and priests to our God;
and we shall reign on the earth."

Although the New International Version translates this song in the third person, the New King James Version of the Bible portrays the elders as human beings; saved by the sacrifice of Jesus: they have been redeemed by the blood of the Lamb. Perhaps further indication that they are indeed the people raised from the dead at the moment of Jesus' death.

In this song is revealed the reason why Jesus alone is eligible to open the scroll. He is the one who was killed for the sins of the world. He is the only Redeemer of the world. Even God the Father and God the Holy Spirit cannot claim these qualifications. And, as it is Jesus' role as Saviour of the world, that allows Him to open the scroll, perhaps what is written on both sides of it are things pertinent to the entire plan of salvation; the mysteries of the plan; the preparations in heaven; Jesus' experience on earth; the history of each person affected by the plan; the roles of the Father and Holy Spirit in the salvation of mankind; the victory gained at the plan's conclusion. Certainly, this would be too much to fit on one side of the scroll.

The heavenly song also celebrates that Christ's sacrifice is for every tribe, language, people and nation. We cannot justify withholding the gospel from anyone. It is for everyone. We cannot discriminate.

God's redeemed will reign on planet earth. Earth will become the new heaven (see Revelation 21:1-3). Wherever God lives is heaven, and when the earth is recreated God will dwell here, thus making the new earth the third heaven where God lives (see 2 Corinthians 12:2-4).

Revelation 5:11-12 - Heaven loves a good sing-a-long. When one group begins to sing the angels cannot help themselves; they must join in. And here, over 100 million angels surround the twenty-four elders and four Cherubim who are circling the Lamb, and begin to sing. The angels cannot sing the song of the redeemed twenty-four elders, for it is not their experience, but they can sing, with all their might, a song of worship and praise. You will recognise the words as those used in one of the anthems of Handel's Messiah - 'Worthy is the Lamb & Amen' (King James Version):

"Worthy is the Lamb, that was slain,
to receive power and riches and wisdom
and strength, and honour, and glory,
and blessing."

Revelation 5:13 – This song is irresistible: all of creation (human and animal) both alive and dead, join in the singing. Listed are those creatures that live both in heaven and on earth, creatures that live on and in the sea, and those who have died. It appears that John, in his vision, has been transported through time to the point when every creature in the universe, whether they are saved or lost, will acknowledge that God is God, and worthy of worship (see Romans 14:11 [KJV]). The list includes every created being; therefore, we must assume the devil and his angels are included. They will at last voluntarily proclaim the unique right of God the Father, and Jesus the Lamb, to be worshiped. It seems safe to assume this extraordinary event will take place just before fire comes down out of heaven to devour the devil, his angels, and the wicked people; as up to this point they refuse to cease their rebellion against God. (We will explore these events fully in Revelation chapter 20). Although the universe has been tarnished by sin, because the majority of earth's inhabitants have chosen to follow Satan rather than God, a time will come when everyone who has ever lived on planet earth, together with all beings in the universe, will accept and proclaim that God is just and worthy of worship. Even the devil, who tried to tempt Jesus to worship him when He was on earth (see Matthew 4:9) will join the adoration. Jesus' response to the devil's temptation was: *"...You shall worship the LORD your God and Him only you shall serve."* (Matthew 9:10). The shoe is now firmly on the other foot; the devil professes that the worship he tried to usurp belongs only to the Godhead.

Here is that momentous song (King James Version):

> *"Blessing, and honour, and glory,*
> *and power, be unto Him*
> *that sitteth upon the throne,*
> *and unto the Lamb for ever and ever."*

Revelation 5:14 – At the singing of the third song the four Cherubim proclaim *"Amen"*. They are satisfied and express their agreement. The question asked in heaven so long ago by Lucifer (now Satan, the devil), concerning who is to be worshiped, has finally been answered by the very person who posed the question and began the controversy, (see Isaiah 14:12-15).

Revelation 5:14 - And of course, as they usually do, the twenty-four elders fall down and worship God.

Revelation Chapter Six

THE FOUR HORSEMEN OF THE APOCALYPSE

Based on Revelation 6:1-17

In Revelation chapters four and five the scene has been dramatically set for the message of chapter six. We know the vision is coming from the throne room of God in the first apartment of the heavenly temple. We have seen the scroll in the hand of God the Father. We know Jesus, the Lamb, our Saviour, will open the scroll. We are now properly prepared to see what happens when the Seven Seals binding the scroll are opened.

Logically, Jesus should simply open all seven seals of the scroll and begin reading, but that does not happen. Each seal is symbolic of a period in history. Just as in chapters two and three, we once again view the seven eras of God's church; from the church of the apostles to the end time church. Therefore, the Seven Seals cover the fate of God's people from the time of the apostolic church to the end of time.

Revelation chapters two and three were messages to the church of Jesus Christ throughout the ages, following His ascension to heaven. They were given to encourage the church and maintain the faith of the brethren. Chapter six is a report on the events and circumstances that impact His church throughout the same time period.

The four horsemen of the Apocalypse appear in this chapter. Traditionally, Revelation 6 has been seen as a foretelling of doom for the earth and its inhabitants, set somewhere in our future. However, when viewed correctly, it is clear the four horsemen depict past eras of the people of God. As a result, we need not fear them. Nevertheless, there is a message for us in this chapter, for the vision transports us through history to the coming of Christ, when the majority of people on earth will be caught unawares and unprepared.

Here is the opening of the Seven Seals. Jesus opens them one by one, and with each opening, a scene is shown which John faithfully describes for us.

Revelation 6:1-2 – Jesus, the Lamb, opens the **First Seal**, and one of the Cherubim invites John to come and see the scene. John sees the first horseman. He is riding a white horse. Everything about this rider signifies victory. He holds a bow, for he is engaged in battle. He is given a crown, or wreath of victory; so already he is a victor. He rides out as a conqueror and more victories are before him.

This then is the apostolic church (AD31-AD100) which in Revelation chapter two is called the church in Ephesus. This was the church begun by Jesus Himself, and continued after His ascension by the disciples who had known Him and been taught by Him. Their understanding of the gospel was pure and untarnished. They had received their message direct from Jesus. They were convinced of their mission to spread the gospel to every nation, kindred, tongue and people (see Matthew 24:14). They had received the gift of the Holy Spirit at Pentecost, therefore completion of the task was assured. Then they believed Jesus would return to take His people to heaven.

The rider on a white horse – a victorious church.

However, Jesus did not return during the time of the apostolic church.

Revelation 6:3-4 – Jesus opens the **Second Seal** and the second Cherubim invites John to watch the next scene. It is the second horseman. He rides a fiery red horse, wealds a large sword, and is given power to deprive the earth of peace by making people kill each other.

It is clear the change of colour of the horse shows a change in the condition of the church of Jesus. No longer is it pure and victorious. Now it is red and causing upheaval, violence and murder. What was happening to the church after AD100? From AD100-AD313 the church was infiltrated by apostasy.

This era of the church coincides with the church of Smyrna in Revelation chapter two: the Persecuted Church. This church rides a red horse (the colour of blood), and in Isaiah 1:18 the colour red is associated with sin. It appears God's church is here shown as overtaken by sin and bloodshed. And indeed, after the death of the original apostles, the church came under fierce attack, as those who held to the undiluted truth were persecuted and put to death by so-called Christians bringing false doctrine into the church. At this time, the Roman Empire sought to marry State and religion as it moved from its pagan phase to its Papal phase. The Roman Christian Church, whilst claiming to be a religious power, was in reality State run and therefore wielded political power. It caused all who did not adhere to its teaching to be persecuted and even killed.

The rider on a red horse – a divided church; waring against itself.

Revelation 6:5-6 – Jesus opens the **Third Seal**, and the third Cherubim invites John to come and look. Out rides the third horseman on a black horse. He is carrying a pair of scales. One of the Cherubim pronounces *"Two pounds of wheat for a day's wages, and six pounds of barley for a day's wages, and do not damage the oil and the wine!"*

This seal must cover the church during AD313-AD538. At this time, the true church of Christ, identified in Revelation chapter two as the church of Pergamum, was losing its battle against Roman infiltration, as the transformation from Pagan Rome to Papal Rome was reaching completion. The white horse has turned to black; the church has become the opposite of its original state.   Under the rule of Roman Emperor, Constantine, Christianity became the State religion, and pagans were bribed to become baptised converts, bringing with them their pagan doctrines, such as:

- Worship on the first day of the week instead of the seventh day, as instituted by God at creation;
- Worship of idols - prohibited by the Ten Commandments;
- Celibacy of the priesthood - a non-biblical practice;
- Burning of candles for the dead - a non-biblical practice;
- Purgatory - a non-biblical doctrine;
- A present hell fire that burns throughout eternity – a non-biblical doctrine;
- Mass – a non-biblical practice;
- Original sin – a non-biblical doctrine.

(www.revelationbibleprophecy.org/revelation6)

The pronouncement of the Cherubim is interesting; it appears the church has become a shopkeeper, using scales to weigh staple food items and sell them at exorbitant prices. This image fits well with the behaviour of the Papal Church at this time. It grew rich on its sale of relics to the masses. People paid to rescue their deceased loved ones out of Purgatory, and large sums were collected by the priests for:

- the forgiveness of sins;
- baptism;
- marriage;
- confirmation;
- burial.

Every spiritual requirement was now for sale. And salvation, the basic need of every human being, offered freely by God to everyone who believes (see John 3:16), became available only to those able to pay. In this way, the church became rich, and the people impoverished.

However, the Cherubim also says, *". . . and do not damage the oil and the wine!"* Whilst the church is making religious necessities unattainable to the poor, some things will remain intact and available. Oil is often used in the Bible to show the work of the Holy Spirit (see Isaiah 61:1, Acts 10:38). During the last supper, Jesus stated the wine was symbolic of His blood that provided forgiveness of sins (see Matthew 26:28). Therefore, the Cherubim is assuring us that although, at this time, the church appears to be overrun by apostasy, a few will remain, led by the Holy Spirit, who maintain belief in the forgiveness of sins through the shed blood of Jesus. The truth will be preserved.

The rider on a black horse – the church becomes a wealthy shopkeeper; religion for sale.

Revelation 6:7-8 – Jesus opens the **Fourth Seal,** and the fourth Cherubim gives John the invitation to come and see.   John sees the fourth horseman riding a pale horse. This rider is called Death, and Hades (the grave) follows close behind him. The rider and Hades are given power to kill people both by the sword and by wild beasts, and to bring famine and plague to a quarter of the earth.

AD538 – 1517 was the time when the Papal Church operated at its height until the beginning of the Reformation (the religious awakening).   During this period, the Roman Catholic Church, through various regimes such as the Spanish Inquisition, tortured and killed an estimated 60,000,000 opposers of its doctrines, by methods that included the sword, starvation, burnings at the stake, the rack, and the use of wild animals. This was certainly a time of death and the grave.   It is interesting that the NIV Bible translation includes plague as a weapon used to bring about death. Biological warfare is perhaps seen as a modern weapon, but historically, Bubonic plague was identified as spread by rats.   It is feasible that infected rats were used to torture enemies of the Catholic Church.

It is said that during this time the Catholic Church ruled one quarter of the then known world. (www.revelationbibleprophecy.org/revelation6) This fact was prophesied in the message of the pale horse.

The rider on a pale horse – the Catholic Church distinguishes itself as a mass murderer.

Revelation 6:9-11 – Jesus opens the **Fifth Seal**. No horse this time. Instead, John sees a representation of the Christians martyred for their faith. Although dead, they cry out for justice, as Abel did after he was murdered by Cain (see Genesis 4:10). As far as God is concerned, all those murdered unjustly, figuratively demand justice from Him. The martyrs cry out *"How long, Sovereign Lord, holy and true, until you judge the inhabitants of the earth and avenge our blood?"* God responds by giving them their white robes. White robes are given to those who are saved (see Revelation 3:5). Clearly, the white robes are a promise of salvation, but the martyrs cannot receive eternal life just yet. They must wait *"a little longer"*, for there are future believers, both men and women, who will also lose their lives for the faith.

A Bible truth is being confirmed here. All God's people will receive their reward together. The righteous do not go straight to heaven when they die. When Jesus returns to the earth for His people, He will collect both those who have died and those still alive, and they will travel to heaven together (see 1 Thessalonians 4:13-18).

Also, God will avenge all the deaths of the innocent. He will finally bring judgement on the wicked; we just need to be patient and trust Him to do so.

The Fifth Seal covers the period 1517-1755; the start of the great Reformation when reformers such as Martin Luther, (a German Catholic monk), John Calvin (a French theologian), Huldrych Zwingli (a Swiss theologian), and others, publicly protested against the Roman Catholic Church, exciting its wrath. Many protestors were hunted down, tortured and murdered, but as a result of their protest the Bible was translated from Latin into the common languages of Europe, enabling ordinary people to read it for themselves. The reformers also spearheaded the new churches of the Protestant Movement, set up in opposition to the Roman Catholic Church.

Revelation 6:12-13 – Jesus opens the **Sixth Seal** which begins at 1755 and ushers in the Time of the End (1798) to the Second Advent. John sees a great earthquake; the sun turns black; the moon shines blood red; the stars fall from the sky.

The Sixth Seal introduces the end time, the time in which we now live. We will find in Revelation that 'time of the end' events are not symbolic. When John sees end time happenings, they are real events, no longer concealed in symbols. The Sixth Seal is a good example. Under this seal John sees four natural phenomena: signs of the times that confirm we are now in the time of the end:

- **A great earthquake.** Here is a quotation from Uriah Smith's 'Daniel and the Revelation', page 414.

  "The great Lisbon earthquake of Nov. 1, 1755, extended over a tract of at least 4,000,000 square miles. Its effects were even extended to the waters in many places, where the shocks were not perceptible. It pervaded the greater portion of Europe, Africa, and America; but its extreme violence was exercised on the south western part of the former. In Africa, this earthquake was felt almost as severely as it had been in Europe. A great part of Algiers was destroyed………… Similar effects were realized at Morocco. Its effects were likewise felt at Tangier, at Tetuan, at Funchal in the Island of Madeira. It is probable that all Africa was shaken. At the north, it extended to Norway and Sweden, Germany, Holland, France, Great Britain, and Ireland were all more or less agitated by the same great commotion of the elements. Lisbon (Portugal), previous to the earthquake in 1755, contained 150,000 inhabitants. Mr Barretti says that 90,000 persons were lost on that fatal day."

- **The sun turned black like sackcloth made of goat hair.** Here is a quotation from 'Webster's Unabridged Dictionary', edition of 1884, page 1604.

  "Dark Day, The May 19, 1780; so called on account of a remarkable darkness on that day, extending over all New England. In some places,

persons could not see to read common print in the open air for several hours together. Birds sang their evening song, disappeared, and became silent; fowls went to roost; cattle sought the barn-yard; and candles were lighted in the houses. The obscuration began about ten o'clock in the morning, and continued till the middle of the next night, but with differences of degree and duration in different places. For several days previous, the wind had been variable, but chiefly from the southwest and the northeast. The true cause of this remarkable phenomenon is not known."

- **The whole moon turned blood red.**
  Mr Tenney, from Exeter, gave the following eye witness account to the Historical Society. It is his experience of the effects of the blood red moon which followed the dark day:

"The darkness of the following evening was probably as gross as has ever been observed since the Almighty first gave birth to light. I could not help conceiving at the time that if every luminous body in the universe had been shrouded in the impenetrable darkness, or struck out of existence, the darkness could not have been more complete. A sheet of white paper held within a few inches of the eyes, was equally invisible with the blackest velvet."

(www.revelationbibleprophecy.org/revelation6)

- **The stars in the sky fell to earth, as figs drop from a fig tree when shaken by a strong wind.**
  Here is a quotation from 'Our First Century', R M Devens, page 32, of the meteor shower of 13 November 1833.

"Extensive and magnificent showers of shooting stars have been known to occur at various places in modern times; but the most universal and wonderful which has ever been recorded, is that of the 13th of November,

1833, the whole firmament, over all the United States, being then, for hours, in fiery commotion. No celestial phenomenon has ever occurred in this country, since its first settlement, which was viewed with such intense admiration by one class in the community, or with so much dread and alarm by another. . . During the three hours of its continuance, the day of judgment was believed to be only waiting for sunrise."

The above quotations give accounts of the fulfilment of Revelation 6:12,13. All the prophesied events took place during the Sixth Seal period:

- 1755 – The Lisbon earthquake;
- 1780 – The sun turned black;
- 1780 – The moon shone blood red;
- 1833 – The stars fell from the sky.

They were God given signs that the earth was entering the time of the end.

Revelation 6:14-17 – The next wonder seen by John under the Sixth Seal is the coming of Jesus, which further confirms that the earthquake and signs shown in the sun, moon and stars are heralds of the end time era during which Jesus will return to earth. John describes how it will happen:

"The heavens receded like a scroll being rolled up, and every mountain and island was removed from its place. Then the kings of the earth, the princes, the generals, the rich, the mighty, and everyone else, both slave and free, hid in caves and among the rocks of the mountains. They called to the mountains and the rocks, 'Fall on us and hide us from the face of Him who sits on the throne and from the wrath of the Lamb! For the great day of their wrath has come, and who can withstand it?'"

What a day that will be. Jesus comes to rescue His people. They have been treated abominably through the ages; hounded, imprisoned, tortured in

65

terrible ways, and murdered, because they would not give up their faith to follow man-made doctrines. Now Jesus turns up to mete out justice. Now it is the rich and powerful men of earth who are running and hiding, desperately trying to avoid facing God the Father, and His Son. This will be a fearful time for those who have refused to follow Jesus. At that time, it does not matter whether they are rich or poor, slave or free. What does matter is whom they have chosen to worship. For those who have given their lives to Jesus, this is a great day of deliverance. For those who have not, this is a frightening day of retribution. Which group we fall into will be determined by the choice we make.

As the Sixth Seal begins in 1755 and extends to the coming of Jesus, we are now living under this seal. In fact, we are presently situated somewhere between verse 13 and verse 14 of Revelation chapter six, for the four great signs of Jesus' coming have taken place, and now we await the event itself.

The chapter ends with the Sixth Seal. As we know, the heavenly scroll has seven seals. We are going to have to wait a little longer for the Seventh Seal to be opened, because Jesus 'sticks a pin' here. He has something to reveal to us before He opens the Seventh Seal. Chapter seven forms a hiatus between the Sixth and Seventh Seals.

Footnote:

In Matthew 24:29-35, sixty years before John received the visions of Revelation, Jesus confirmed all that John sees in the opening of the Sixth Seal. Jesus predicts the signs of His second coming. He refers to the sun being darkened, the moon not giving its light, and the stars falling from the sky as the heavenly bodies are shaken. Then He says, the Son of Man will appear, and the peoples of the earth will mourn when they see Him.

Whilst on earth, Jesus warned us of the signs heralding the nearness of His coming. In Matthew 24 He tells us to watch for these signs. Sixty years later, He repeats His declaration to John in Revelation 6:12-17, and instructs him to record it. Surely, this is an important message, and one we need to heed. Jesus wants us to be in the right group, the group that will welcome Him when He comes. Clearly, He is doing all He can to save us from being in the group that will run away from Him, seeking death rather than to look in His face. None of us need be in the second group; we have received ample warning.

Revelation Chapter Seven

THE 144,000

Based on Revelation 7:1-17

Revelation chapter seven interrupts the Seven Seals. It comes after the Sixth Seal, showing the second coming of Jesus, and before the Seventh Seal, because it answers the question asked at the end of chapter six *"For the great day of their wrath has come, and who can withstand it?"* (Revelation 6:17). Chapter seven tells us who can withstand the second coming of Christ: the answer is - The 144,000.

Revelation 7:1 – We are taken back to the time just before Jesus' coming. John sees four angels standing at the four compass points of the earth: North, South, East and West. They are desperately straining to hold back the four winds of the earth; preventing them from blowing on the land, sea or trees. Obviously, disaster is coming. Under the Sixth Seal we saw the planet ravaged by the coming of Jesus. Yet even before this event, troubled times are predicted that will threaten the people on earth. In Bible prophecy, destructive winds blowing on the earth represent God's judgement on the nations (see Jeremiah 25:31,32). It appears that in the end time, before Jesus comes, the world will experience the wrath of God, which will physically harm our planet.

However, at this point, God's angels are holding back the winds of strife.

Few people comprehend the restraining power of God. Mankind has been brought to the brink of disaster many times through war, such as during both the First and Second World Wars, industrial accidents, such as the Chernobyl nuclear power plant fire, man's continued destructive practices leading to climate change and irreversible pollution of our planet, the nuclear threat as more and more countries develop atomic weapons. Yet God is holding back the winds of strife so that we do not destroy ourselves. Nevertheless, a time will come when the desire of men to annihilate one another, and the planet on which they live, will no longer be held in check by a loving God. He will remove all constraints, and people will then witness a world left to its own evil devices. It will be a fearful time, one followed by the wrath of God Himself, who will bring punishment on the wicked people of the earth.

But before the winds of men's strife, and God's wrath, are let loose, something needs to be done; God's people must be shielded.

Revelation 7:2-3 – John sees another angel flying in from the east. He is carrying the *"seal of the living God"* and he calls out in a loud voice to the four angels holding back the winds *"Do not harm the land or the sea or the trees until we put a seal on the foreheads of the servants of our God."* God's people are to be sealed. In other words, they are to be protected from the coming tumult.

The angel proclaims they are to be sealed on their foreheads. When we come to Revelation 14, we will see that the seal of God is identified as the name of Jesus and God the Father.

In Jeremiah 31:33,34 we are told God will put His law *".. in their minds and write it on their hearts"*. This, of course, is symbolic language describing the intellectual and emotional connection between God and His people, explained later in the chapter (verse 34) when God says His people will *". . .all know Me"*.

Therefore, in Revelation 7 when God's people are sealed on their foreheads with the name of Jesus and God the Father, once again, a symbolic reference is being made, indicating that God's people, at the end of time, will possess a deep knowledge of Jesus borne out of sincere love that designates them as His own. This is a purposeful, intentional, relationship they have thought through, and committed to. They have decided to belong to Jesus. They are His, and therefore can now be sealed in their decision. The great destruction to come on the earth, before Christ's return, will not harm them.

It is interesting that in Jeremiah 31:33,34, it is His law that God writes in the hearts and minds of His people. Thus, their relationship with God consists of knowing Him (the mind), and loving Him (the heart), and consequently they keep His law. Keeping God's law is the sign of their love relationship with Him (see 1 John 5:3). Therefore, it could be said that having the seal of God is demonstrated through obedience to God's law, and this is what differentiates His people from everyone else on earth at the end of time.

God's law (the Ten Commandments) is recorded in Exodus 20. Within the law, there is one commandment that has the hallmarks of a seal. It is the fourth commandment that instructs us to keep holy the seventh day of the week as a memorial of creation (see Exodus 20:8-11). In ancient times, a king would identify himself and his authority through his seal. The seal was the mark or sign of his nobility and rulership. It would usually contain the name, title and territory of the ruler.

Here is the fourth commandment:
"Remember the Sabbath day by keeping it holy. Six days you shall labour and do all your work, but the seventh day is a Sabbath to the Lord your God. On it you shall not do any work, neither you, nor your son or daughter, nor your male or female servant, nor your animals, nor any foreigner residing in your towns. For in six days the Lord made the heavens and the earth, the sea, and all that

is in them, but He rested on the seventh day. Therefore the Lord blessed the Sabbath day and made it holy." (Exodus 20:8-11)

In this commandment we see all the features of a seal:

- The Name of the Ruler – **The Lord your God**;
- His Title – **Creator of the heavens, earth, sea, and all the beings that inhabit them**;
- His Territory – **The heavens and earth (The Universe)**.

In effect, our relationship with God, signified by our keeping of the Ten Commandments sincerely, because we love Him, is the seal of God. The fourth commandment especially shows this seal. God's seal does not need to be a literal/visible mark; it is an intellectual and emotional decision, evidenced by obedience to God's law, thus designating God's people as belonging to Him. God's ownership of His people is visible in their behaviour.

Revelation 7:4 – The number of the sealed people on earth, who are faithful to God at the time just before Jesus comes, is given. There are 144,000. There has been much speculation regarding whether this is a literal or symbolic number. Nevertheless, when we consider that these are the total number of righteous people alive when Jesus comes, this seems a relatively small group, if taken literally. Could it be that out of the billions of people alive on earth, only 144,000 will be saved? Also, when looking at the number itself, it is interesting that it is made up of multiples of 12.

As we have already discovered in the book of Revelation, numbers are significant. We know that seven signifies perfection and completeness, because it shows the workings of God (signified by 3) on man (signified by 4), thus, 3 + 4 = 7. Twelve also shows perfection and completeness, thus, 3 x 4 = 12. Therefore, 144,000, which is 12 x 12,000, could signify a multitude of perfect, complete or righteous people. In other words, a large group of God's people. A symbolic view of the number would fit with the fact that we are dealing with prophecy, and in prophecy numbers are usually symbolic.

The angel says the 144,000 will be sealed from all the tribes of Israel. One view is that only those born of Israeli parentage will be saved when Jesus comes. However, this seems unlikely, as Jesus instructed His disciples that the gospel should be taken to every nation (see Matthew 24:14). There would be no point in preaching to every nation if only Israelites will be saved.

It is logical to conclude that Revelation 7 is referring to the symbolic or spiritual tribes of Israel. The idea that those who follow Jesus (whether Jew or Gentile) are designated as 'spiritual Israel' is not a new one. In Galatians 3:26-29 Paul explains that once a person (whether Jew or Gentile) accepts Jesus into their life, they become an heir of the promise given to Abraham; therefore, they become part of Abraham's seed. The promise was that the Messiah would come through Abraham's lineage, and through Him, all nations on earth would be blessed (see Genesis 18:18). Therefore, being a follower of Jesus designates one as a member of spiritual Israel; spiritually Abraham's seed.

Moreover, as we are considering one group, and the number of people that make up the group is symbolic, it stands to reason that the classification of the group's lineage is also symbolic. We are looking at a symbol; the 144,000 are a large group of righteous people, who have accepted Jesus into their lives, and are obedient to the law of God. Each member of this group will receive the seal of God, which will protect them from His wrath soon to come on the earth.

Revelation 7:5-8 – The angel gives a list of exactly how the number of the 144,000 is made up. They come from each of the twelve tribes of Israel: 12,000 from each tribe, as follows:
- 12,000 from Judah
- 12,000 from Reuben
- 12,000 from Gad

- 12,000 from Asher
- 12,000 from Naphtali
- 12,000 from Manasseh
- 12,000 from Simeon
- 12,000 from Levi
- 12,000 from Issachar
- 12,000 from Zebulun
- 12,000 from Joseph
- 12,000 from Benjamin

Remember, these are symbolic numbers and tribes, so we need to decipher just why these tribes are listed in this way, for it is certainly significant.

First, the fact that there are 12,000 from each tribe signifies large groups of righteous people (as shown above). But let us look at the tribes themselves.

The literal twelve tribes of Israel were the descendants of the twelve sons of Jacob, whose name was changed to Israel (see Genesis 32:28). The sons are listed in Genesis 46 as:
- Reuben
- Simeon
- Levi
- Judah
- Issachar
- Zebulun
- Gad
- Asher
- Joseph
- Benjamin
- Dan
- Naphtali

If we compare this list with the list in Revelation 7, we will see some differences. For example, the lists are in a different order. The Genesis list puts Jacob's sons in age order, grouped under the wife who bore them (Jacob had two wives and two concubines who were the maids of his two wives). However, the list in Revelation 7 puts Judah first, and replaces Dan with Manasseh. Manasseh was the son of Joseph (Jacob's grandson). When Jacob, at the end of his life, pronounced blessings on his sons, instead of blessing Joseph, he gave the blessing to Joseph's two sons, Ephraim and Manasseh. As a result, they were incorporated into the twelve tribes as two half tribes. It is curious, therefore, that in the list of the twelve tribes to be sealed at the end of time, Dan is omitted, Manasseh (one of the half tribes) is included, Joseph is included, and the second half tribe, Ephraim, is omitted. As with everything in Revelation, this must be significant.

Here are two suggestions for the amended list in Revelation 7.

In Genesis 49 each of the twelve tribes is given one or more characteristic:

Tribe	Characteristic	Bible Reference
Judah	Ruler. Warrior.	Genesis 49:8-10
Reuben	Lost his leadership role because he was sexually immoral.	Genesis 49:3,4
Gad	Oppressed and beaten but gets revenge in any way he can.	Genesis 49:19
Asher	He likes to eat rich food.	Genesis 49:20
Naphtali	Bears beautiful children.	Genesis 49:21
Manasseh	He is faithful. He keeps his word and acts with honour and responsibility.	Joshua 1:12-15
Simeon	Violent.	Genesis 49:5-7
Levi	Violent.	Genesis 49:5-7
Issachar	Lazy.	Genesis 49:14-15
Zebulun	Seafarer.	Genesis 49:13
Joseph	Steady, strong and blessed.	Genesis 49:22-26
Benjamin	Ravenous wolf – a wild one who likes to fight and conquer.	Genesis 49:27

Those tribes not included in the 144,000 in Revelation 7:

Tribe	Characteristic	Bible Reference
Dan	He is a leader but when people look to him for guidance, they discover he is a deceitful serpent or viper who attacks from the back and causes people to fall backwards.	Genesis 49:17
Ephraim	Proud. Thinking himself superior. Not willing to go out to battle but seeking the glory after the battle is won.	Judges 12:1-7

The list of tribes included in the 144,000 have an assortment of characteristics, some good, some not so good. Yet, they are listed as those who are sealed. This could indicate that whatever our character, Jesus is able to cover us with His blood. Jesus came to save sinners; therefore, there is hope for us all.

What of the two tribes excluded from the 144,000? Their characteristics of being leaders who deceive the brethren and cause them to fall backwards, or, supposed people of God who portray themselves as superior to their brethren, not willing to work but seeking the glory, could be a warning to those amongst God's people who behave in this way, and as a result, will not be saved.

A second suggestion for the significance of the list in Revelation 7 is the story told through the meanings of the tribal names:

Tribe	Meaning of Name	Bible Reference
Judah	Now I will praise the Lord	Genesis 29:35
Reuben	Surely the Lord has looked upon my affliction	Genesis 29:32
Gad	What good fortune	Genesis 30:11
Asher	How happy I am	Genesis 30:13
Naphtali	I have had a great struggle, and won	Genesis 30:8
Manasseh	God has made me forget all my trouble	Genesis 41:51
Simeon	Because the Lord heard that I was hated	Genesis 29:33

Tribe	Meaning of Name	Bible Reference
Levi	Now at last my husband will become attached to me	Genesis 29:34
Issachar	God has rewarded me	Genesis 30:18
Zebulun	God has presented me with a precious gift. My husband will treat me with honour	Genesis 30:20
Joseph	The Lord will add to me	Genesis 30:24
Benjamin	The son of my right hand	Genesis 35:17,18

When the meanings of the tribal names are combined in the order they are listed in Revelation 7, they tell this story:

'Now I shall praise the Lord; for surely He has looked upon my affliction. What good fortune, and how happy I am; I have had a great struggle, and won. And God has made me forget all my trouble, because He has heard that I was hated. Now at last my Husband will become attached to me. God has rewarded me; He has presented me with a precious gift, and my Husband will treat me with honour. The Lord will add to me the Son of my (His) right hand.'

This story certainly resonates with the experience of God's people at the end of time. These people, the 144,000, are sealed to enable them to survive a great time of tribulation that is to come on the earth (also referred to in Daniel 12:1,2). It is a story of deliverance for the people of God; they will be treated with honour by Christ, the Husband of the church (see Ephesians 5:25-27), the Son of God's right hand.

Revelation 7:9-12 – The scene now shifts to heaven. John is shown a multitude that no-one can count. This must be a different group to the 144,000 who are specifically numbered. The uncountable multitude stand before the throne of God wearing white robes. We already know from Revelation 3:5 that it is the redeemed who are given white robes to wear in heaven. We must conclude, then, that this numberless group are the saved of all ages – a group too great to count. As they are before the throne of God, this scene must take place after Jesus has collected both the living and the dead saints from the earth. In other words, this is the victory ceremony in heaven after the Second Advent.

Whereas, the 144,000 are from one nation (symbolic Israel), John identifies the numberless group as coming from *"every nation, tribe, people and language"*. Therefore, John saw people of different colours, hair type, physical characteristics, size, and shape. Isn't it wonderful that in heaven we will keep our diversity? They are holding victory palm branches, and, they are singing:

> *"Salvation belongs to our God,*
> *who sits on the throne*
> *and to the Lamb"*

And the angels, and the twenty-four elders join in with:

> *"Amen!*
> *Praise and glory*
> *and wisdom and thanks and honour*
> *and power and strength*
> *be to our God for ever and ever.*
> *Amen!"*

What a heart-warming scene of rejoicing. The people of God have made it: they are saved.

Revelation 7:13-17 - One of the twenty-four elders draws John's attention back to the special group, the 144,000, who are the subject of this chapter. They are also part of the heavenly victory ceremony, but standing in a separate group to the numberless multitude. He asks John *"These in white robes – who are they and where did they come from?"* John has seen both groups, the

144,000 who receive the end time seal, and the great multitude raised from their graves to meet Jesus at His second coming. However, John cannot answer the elder's question. He does not know why the 144,000 have been singled out in heaven. So he answers *"Sir, you know"*. John doesn't know the answer but he feels the elder does. Fortunately, the elder is able to answer his own question. He says:

"These are they who have come out of the great tribulation; they have washed their robes and made them white in the blood of the Lamb. Therefore they are before the throne of God and serve Him day and night in His temple; and He who sits on the throne will shelter them with His presence. Never again will they hunger; never again will they thirst. The sun will not beat down on them, nor any scorching heat. For the Lamb at the centre of the throne will be their Shepherd; He will lead them to springs of living water. And God will wipe away every tear from their eyes."

Surely, this is confirmation of the story of the 144,000 shown above. This group needs to receive the end time seal in order to endure the terrible tribulation that will come on God's people just before Jesus returns to planet earth. Moreover, we are given hints of what that tribulation will comprise; hunger, thirst, scorching by the sun. Their particular reward will be to serve in the heavenly temple, much like the ancient Levite tribe, that was set apart to serve in the wilderness sanctuary. In addition, the 144,000 will be the special emissaries of Jesus; they will accompany Him wherever He travels. What an honour!

Footnote:

In Revelation chapter fourteen we will meet the 144,000 again. But now we know who they are; they are God's people who are alive when Jesus comes. They will withstand the devastation His coming will cause. They are the ones who are specifically sealed by God to go through the great tribulation just before Jesus' coming. Theirs is an exceptional experience and so they are especially honoured.

Now that the question posed in Revelation 6:17 has been well and truly answered. We can go back to the opening of the seventh and last seal.

Revelation Chapter Eight

THE SEVENTH SEAL AND THE SEVEN TRUMPETS

Based on Revelation 8:1-13

Revelation 6 ends with the opening of the Sixth Seal (Revelation 6:12-17). Under this seal we saw signs in the sun, moon and stars, heralding the coming of Jesus. These signs were fulfilled in the eighteenth and nineteenth centuries. The Sixth Seal also showed the devastation of earth at the Second Coming, and the dramatic reaction of those unprepared for the event. As the Second Coming has not yet taken place, we are presently living within the Sixth Seal, awaiting Jesus' return to earth. Revelation 7 answers the question posed at the end of Revelation 6 *'who will be able to stand at Jesus' coming?'* And we have found that the answer is - The 144,000.

Revelation 8 returns to the opening of the Seven Seals. For there is one seal left unopened.

Revelation 8:1 - The opening of the **Seventh Seal** brings silence in heaven for half-an-hour. As we know, when dealing with Bible prophecy, we must use the prophetic time formula of 'one prophetic day equals one literal year' (see Numbers 14:34, Ezekiel 4:6). In Revelation 8:1 we are given a time period, and as it is prophetic time, we must treat it in the same way. Biblical time periods use the ancient Jewish/Hebrew calendar, known as the Biblical Lunar Calendar (BLC), which governs all Bible chronology.

Half an hour in prophetic time can be calculated as follows:
- One prophetic day equals one literal year.
- In the ancient Jewish calendar (or BLC) one year was made up of 360 days.

- In Revelation 8:1 we are dealing with prophetic hours.
- As one literal hour is $1/24^{th}$ of a literal day, we must find out $1/24^{th}$ of a prophetic day.
- As one prophetic day equals 360 literal days (or one Jewish year), to find $1/24^{th}$ of a prophetic day, we divide 360 (the days in a literal year) by 24 (the hours in one literal day). 360 days divided by 24 equals 15 days.
- Therefore, one prophetic hour equals 15 literal days (15 days are $1/24^{th}$ of 360 days).
- Then to find one prophetic half an hour, we can divide 15 by 2, which equals 7.5 literal days.
- We can also do this calculation by dividing 360 (the days in a year) by 48 (the number of half hours in one day). 360 divided by 48 equals 7.5.
- Therefore, one prophetic half an hour equals 7.5 literal days (7.5 days are $1/48^{th}$ of 360 days, just as one literal half hour is $1/48^{th}$ of a literal day).

The above calculation confirms that in Revelation 8:1 the opening of the Seventh Seal brings about a period of silence in heaven that lasts seven and a half days.

What could cause silence in heaven for seven and a half days? Matthew 16:27 and 25:31 tell us that when Jesus comes back to earth He will be accompanied by His Father and all His holy angels. Therefore, heaven will be empty. There will be silence there.

In Daniel 9 the Angel Gabriel tells Daniel that as soon as he began his 2.5 minute prayer, he (Gabriel) was despatched from God to give an answer. It took less than 2.5 minutes for Gabriel to fly at speed from heaven to earth. So why then is heaven empty for seven and a half days at the coming of Jesus?

We can use our imaginations here. It is clear the Second Advent is a special occasion. We have the whole of heaven travelling together in a monumental celestial caravan, including the Father, Son and millions upon millions of angels (we can assume the Holy Spirit is already on earth concluding His mission [see John 16:7-11]). Let's give the heavenly throng half a day to get here. They arrive, and pick up both the living righteous, and those faithful people who have died through the ages (see 1 Thessalonians 4:16-18). Then, they begin the heaven bound homeward journey. Among this group will be many who are not familiar with Jesus. They have not had the opportunity to get to know Him. They may never have enjoyed worshiping on the Sabbath. They have lived faithful lives, obedient to the moral code they have been taught. They are saved because they have carried out all the good they know, and as we are told in Acts 17:30, God judges us for the things we know, not for the things we do not know. A seven day journey back to heaven would give ample time for some stops along the way; time for a tour around the cosmos, and visits to other inhabited planets, where mankind's progress on earth has been closely followed (see 1 Corinthians 4:9). There will be time to be introduced to Jesus, and to keep one Sabbath day holy. Therefore, all who arrive in heaven will be acquainted with Jesus, their Saviour, and will have worshiped the Creator of the universe on the specific day set aside for this purpose.

It's all speculation of course, the Bible does not tell us why heaven is silent for seven and a half days, but we do know whatever takes place during this time period must concern the Second Advent, and cannot be seven days spent on planet earth after Jesus returns. We will see what happens on earth after the Second Advent in Revelation chapter twenty.

A seven day tour around the universe seems a great idea to me!

Revelation 8:1 ends the Seven Seals.

The Seven Trumpets

Revelation 8:2 – We return to the heavenly sanctuary. John sees the seven angels who stand before God. These angels are given seven trumpets. Each angel will blow his trumpet and with each trumpet blast we will see a scene in history affecting God's people.

Revelation 8:3-4 – But first, in the heavenly sanctuary, John sees an angel performing a priestly function. He is offering incense before the Altar of Incense in the Holy Place. And, as we know that Jesus is our High Priest, who officiates in the heavenly temple on our behalf (see Hebrews 4:14 and 9:11), we can conclude this Angel is Jesus Himself. He is still in the Holy Place. He has not yet entered into the Most Holy Place. Therefore, this scene in Revelation 8 is pre-1844.

In the companion to this book 'An Idiot's Guide to the Book of Daniel' there is a detailed explanation of the 2,300 days prophecy, which explains that on 22 October 1844 Jesus moved from the Holy Place of the heavenly temple to the Most Holy Place where the Investigative Judgement is now taking place. Therefore, in Revelation 8:3, as Jesus is offering incense in the Holy Place of the temple, the scenes we are about to view must take place before 22 October 1844.

Jesus has a golden censer (a container specifically for burning incense), and is offering a great amount of incense mixed with the prayers of all God's people. The smoke produced by the burning incense, together with the prayers, rise before God. Jesus is carrying out His mediatorial duty (see 1 Timothy 2:5). On earth, the saints of God are praying, and in heaven, Jesus is mediating on their behalf. Only in this way can God the Father answer their prayers. It appears the saints are praying for God to bring retribution on their behalf, for, in answer to their prayers judgements take place.

Revelation 8:5 – Suddenly Jesus fills the censer with fire and hurls it down to the earth, and thunder, rumblings, lightning and an earthquake are the result.

What we will find is, the seven trumpet blasts will herald judgements on those who have persecuted the saints of God. In Bible times trumpet blasts often signified warnings of battle and destruction (see Jeremiah 4:19-21). Rome was the world-ruling empire at the time John was writing the book of Revelation. The seven angels, who blow the Seven Trumpets, proclaim that the power of Rome will suffer retribution and destruction: it is 'pay-back' time for this major persecutor of God's people.

Revelation 8:6-7 – The seven angels now prepare to blow their trumpets. The first angel blows, and in heaven appears hail and fire mixed with blood, which are thrown down on the earth, and a third of the earth, trees and green grass is burned up.

Following the rule of Emperor Constantine, the Roman Empire was divided into three parts (East, West and the central section call Illyricum). We know from history that the fall of the Roman Empire began with the overthrow of the western section.

Revelation 8 deals with the first four trumpets, and we will see several references to 'a third' being destroyed. It is clear that in this chapter John is firstly witnessing the destruction of the western section of the Roman Empire. Regarding the means of Rome's destruction (hail, fire and blood), we can look to another Bible prophecy in Isaiah 28:2, where God warned Israel it would be attacked by a kingdom from the north, Assyria, which is described as being *"like a hailstorm"*. Similarly, the early attacks on Rome described as *"hail"* came from the north. Gothic (or Germanic) tribes ruled by Alaric reined terror on the western Roman territory from AD395-AD428. Alaric used fire to burn entire villages and their farm land, and massacred the populace. Hence, John's description of fire mixed with blood that destroyed the earth, trees and grass.

Yet, only a third is destroyed, because the main area of Alaric's attacks was the western part of the Roman Empire.

('The Decline and Fall of the Roman Empire', Edward Gibbon, Volume 3, Chapter 30, page 253)

Revelation 8:8-9 – The second angel blows his trumpet and something that looks like a huge, burning mountain is thrown into the sea. As a result, a third of the sea turns to blood, a third of the creatures in the sea die, and a third of the ships are destroyed.

We must turn to other parts of the Bible to interpret these images. In Jeremiah 51:25 the ancient kingdom of Babylon is described as a destroying and burned-out mountain. This imagery ties in well with John's vision, leading us to conclude that the huge burning mountain, he sees hurled into the sea, is a great, destroying nation engaging in sea battles.

The one Gothic tribe that attacked the Roman Empire by sea was the Vandals ruled by Genseric. A group of Gothic tribes such as the Vandals, Visigoths, Burgundians and Suevi joined forces to attack and settle in various parts of Europe, leaving the Vandals to cross into Northern Africa; the western Rome province, besieging it along its coastline in AD439 (www.revelationbibleprophecy.org/revelation8). The naval battles, involving the Vandals, caused great bloodshed and destruction. The Roman naval fleet was decimated, and much of the empire's food supply was cut off. As this happened in the western territory of Rome, once again John writes that only a third of creatures and ships were destroyed.

Revelation 8:10-11 – When the third angel blows his trumpet a great star, blazing like a torch, falls from the sky on a third of the rivers and springs of water. The star has a name; it is called Wormwood. A third of the drinking water turns bitter and, as a result, people die from drinking the water.

Again, let us turn to another part of the Bible to identify this *"great star called Wormwood"*. In the book of Jude, certain ungodly leaders who pervert the truth are called *"wandering [or shooting] stars"* (see Jude 12,13). A shooting star is a meteor showing sudden and temporary brilliance. And, the meaning of the name Wormwood is 'bitterness'. Therefore, this great star appears to be a great leader who comes suddenly on the scene, shines brilliantly for a short period, before fading, and who spreads bitterness wherever he goes.

One very intense, but short reign was that of Attila the Hun (AD451-AD453). His rule was characterised by the great amount of slaughter committed by the Huns, and Attila himself. Attila was notoriously aggressive and ruthless. He was known for personally killing many of his own men. He killed his brother in order to gain full control over the Huns, and his was indeed a short and bitter reign. The Hun onslaught caused a domino effect. They attacked from the east, pushing the Goths further west, who then, being attacked by the Huns on one side, pressed into the Western Roman Empire. (Wikipedia – Attila the Hun)

You will notice, the bitter star (Attila) falls into drinking water and kills everyone who drinks it; surely symbolic of his deadly effect on everyone with whom he came into contact, whether they were his enemies, his countrymen or his own family. Effectively, everyone who shared his drinking water, died.

Revelation 8:12 – The fourth angel blows his trumpet and a third of the sun, moon and stars are turned dark, causing a third of both the day and night to lose their light.

John is still seeing 'a third' being affected, so we are still dealing with the fall of the Western Roman Empire. Under the blowing of the Third Trumpet, we saw a shooting star symbolising a leader. Similarly, under the Fourth Trumpet we see heavenly bodies, including stars. We could, then, look for leaders who these heavenly bodies might represent. The leaders are not attacking or destroying, they are simply turning dark and not shedding light. So perhaps these leaders are not external to Rome, but within Rome itself: Roman leaders. Rome was led by three levels of government, as follows:

- The Emperor (the Sun)
- The Consuls (the Moon)
- The Senate (the Stars)

The last Western Roman Emperor, Romulus Augustulus, reigned from AD476 – AD500.

The Roman Consulship was extinguished in AD541.

The Roman Senate was banished in AD553.

All three levels of western Roman government went dark under the blowing of the Fourth Trumpet.

Revelation 8:13 – Now John sees an eagle, flying in mid-air. The eagle begins to shout a message. In the Old Testament, an eagle flying, ready to swoop, was symbolic of pending disaster (see Hosea 8:1 and Habakkuk 1:8,9). Therefore, we should not expect a positive message from this eagle. The message is *"Woe! Woe! Woe to the inhabitants of the earth, because of the trumpet blasts about to be sounded by the other three angels!"*

We have witnessed the devastation of the Western Roman Empire under the first four trumpets, but now we are being warned; the next three trumpets are going to be much, much worse. 'Woe' can be translated as misery, sorrow, distress or sadness. All these are to come, as we move to Revelation chapter nine and the decline of the Eastern Roman Empire.

Revelation Chapter Nine

THE FIRST TWO WOES (Fifth and Sixth Trumpets)

Based on Revelation 9:1-21

In Revelation chapter nine we see the continuation of the Seven Trumpets, which are God's judgements on the Roman Empire: God is repaying this empire for its persecution of His people.

In Revelation 8 we saw the first four trumpets, cataloguing the destruction of the Western Roman Empire, which by AD476 was totally extinguished. Now we will concentrate on the Eastern Roman Empire after AD476.

The Fifth Trumpet (Revelation 9:1-12)

Revelation 9:1 - When the fifth angel sounds his trumpet a star falls from the sky to the earth. As in Revelation 8:10, we can identify a 'fallen star' as a fallen or corrupt leader (see Jude 12,13). This corrupt leader is given the key to the shaft of the Abyss, or the bottomless pit. In other words, he is given the power to open the 'Abyss' (Greek word 'Abussos'). The Hebrew equivalent of Abussos is Tehom, which again means an abyss or bottomless pit. In Genesis 1:2, the earth, in its original dark and empty state before God began His work of creation, is described as a 'Tehom'. Also, in Jeremiah 4:23-26, Tehom describes the earth after the destruction caused by Jesus' coming (see Revelation 6:14), when the wicked have been slain by the brightness of His coming (see 2 Thessalonians 2:8), and the righteous have been transported to heaven (see 1 Thessalonians 4:16,17). Thus, the earth reverts to its original construction - formless, dark and void.

The bottomless pit or 'Abyss' in Revelation 9:1 is a description of the earth in a desolate state. (We will come back to the precise location of this particular bottomless pit.)

Revelation 9:2 - When the fallen leader opens the Abyss smoke comes out of it, like smoke from a gigantic furnace that darkens the sun and sky. The effect of this smoke is to blot out the source of light and bring darkness.

Throughout the Bible, the Word of God is described as being light and/or truth (see Psalms 119:105, John 17:17), and evil and error described as darkness (see John 3:19, 1 Peter 2:9)

These texts help us understand that the smoke, which comes out of the Abyss, is evil and error, for it brings darkness that blots out the light. The fallen leader releases evil and error in order to blot out the truth of Jesus Christ.

Revelation 9:3 - Out of the smoke (evil and error) come locusts given the power of scorpions. In the book of Daniel we are told that prophetic beasts represent kingdoms (see Daniel 7:17). The large beasts in Daniel's visions represent world ruling kingdoms. Locusts, extremely small beasts, represent many small kingdoms. And, as we shall see, these prophetic locusts are strange creatures.

We know that locusts, in the natural world, gather in swarms and devour all vegetation in their path. The locusts in Revelation 9:3 have tails like scorpions. Again, in the natural world, scorpions use their tails to give a painful, sometimes deadly, sting. These prophetic locusts not only devour their enemies, but also carry a sting in their tails. Here, we can refer to another prophecy in Isaiah 9:14,15 where 'tails' are likened to *"prophets who teach lies"*.

The above helps us identify these uncommon locusts; they are a confederation of small nations, attacking as a swarm, devouring their enemies, not only by force of numbers, but also by the doctrine of deceiving prophets, in an attempt to blot out truth.

Revelation 9:4 - The kingdoms, emerging from the Abyss (a place of desolation), are not allowed to harm the grass of the earth, nor any plant, nor tree, but only those people who do not have the seal of God on their foreheads, that is, those who do not have a saving relationship with God. Therefore, the attacking kingdoms will be restricted: they cannot destroy the vegetation, nor can they hurt the followers of God.

Let us look in history to see who these locust kingdoms are.

The fallen leader with the key to the bottomless pit:

An apostate leader who fits the description is Chosroes II. He was restored to the Persian throne in AD591 and ruled until AD628, at which time one of his sons murdered him. It was the aim of Chosroes to restore Persia as world ruler by attacking the Eastern Roman Empire.

"Through his conquests against the Romans, Chosroes, exhausted his own kingdom. But at the same time, in repelling the attack, Heraclius (King of the Arabs) exhausted his. Through his conquests both nations were exhausted and thus Chosroes had opened the way, (the desolate wasteland, where the Arabs live), for the Arabs to begin to take over." ('Decline and Fall of the Roman Empire', Edward Gibbon, volume 5, chapter 46, page 42)

Bottomless Pit:

The bottomless pit that was opened by Chosroes II, is the desolate wastelands of Arabia.

Locusts:

In other parts of the Bible, locusts symbolise the numerous Arabian tribes. Judges 6:5; 7:12, tell of the Midianite and Amalekite Arabs, *"They came up with their livestock and their tents like swarms of locusts. It was impossible to count them or their camels; they invaded the land to ravage it." "The Midianites, the Amalekites and all the other eastern people had settled in the valley, thick as locusts. . . "*

The Midianites and Amalekites were the Arabian tribes of the east described as locusts because of their numbers. The Arabs consisted of many small tribes, that when combined, became like a swarm of locusts.

It is also interesting to note that the locust was the national emblem of the Ishmaelites, descendants of Abraham's first son, and one of the largest Arab tribes. (www.revelationbibleprophecy.org/revelation9)

Moreover, in the time of Moses, one of the plagues poured out on Egypt was a plague of locusts, which was blown into Egypt by an east wind from Arabia (see Exodus 10:13).

Smoke - Power as scorpions:

We have already seen that the smoke coming out of the Abyss is a reference to evil and error, and that the Arabian tribe's (locust's) power is in its scorpion tail, which we found to be a symbol of a deceiving prophet. So here we have the Arabian tribes, led by a deceiving prophet, attacking the Eastern Roman Empire in great numbers. The prophet of the Arabian tribes was Mohammed.

Mohammed was born in AD569 in Mecca, and died on the 8 June AD632. His teachings could certainly be viewed as fanatical. Here are three quotations from Gibbon's 'Decline and Fall of the Roman Empire' (volume 5, chapter 50, page 332). They outline Mohammed's attacks on Rome; his description of the pleasures of paradise; and his teachings regarding those who fight for Islam.

Quotation 1 – Mohammed's attacks on Rome:

"While the state, (that is Eastern Rome), was exhausted by the Persian war, and the church was distracted by the Nestorian and Monophysite sects,

Mahomet [Mohammed], with sword in one hand and the Koran in the other, erected his throne on the ruins of Christianity and of Rome. The genius of the Arabian prophet, the manners of his nation, and the spirit of his [Mohammed's] religion involve the causes of the decline and fall of the Eastern empire; and our eyes are curiously intent on one of the most memorable revolutions which have impressed a new and lasting character on the nations of the globe."

Quotation 2 – Mohammed describes paradise:

"*Seventy-two* Houris, *or black-eyed girls of resplendent beauty, blooming youth, virgin purity, and exquisite sensibility, will be created for the use of the meanest believer; a moment of pleasure will be prolonged to a thousand years, and his faculties will be increased an hundred-fold, to render him worthy of his felicity.*"

Quotation 3 – Mohammed's teachings on the rewards granted to those fighting for Islam:

"*From all sides the roving Arabs were allured to the standard of religion and plunder; the apostle sanctified the license of embracing the female captives as their wives or concubines; and the enjoyment of wealth and beauty was a feeble type of the joys of paradise prepared for the valiant martyrs of the faith. 'The sword,' says Mahomet [Mohammed], 'is the key of heaven and of hell: a drop of blood shed in the cause of God, a night spent in arms, is of more avail than two months of fasting or prayer: whosoever falls in battle, his sins are forgiven; at the day of judgment his wounds shall be resplendent as vermillion, and odoriferous as musk; and the loss of his limbs shall be supplied by the wings of angels and cherubim.'*"

Mohammed's teachings opposed those of the Bible. He therefore fits the description of obscuring the light of the truth with evil and error. Here are some of his teachings compared with Bible truth:

Mohammed says:	The Bible says:
Jesus is only a prophet;	Jesus is God (John 1:1);
Jesus did not die for our sins. Therefore, there is no salvation for mankind;	Jesus died for our sins and through His death we gain eternal life (Hebrews 9:14,15,28);
The Koran replaces the Bible;	The Bible is the inspired word of God (2 Timothy 3:16);
Friday replaces the seventh-day Sabbath as the day of worship;	The seventh-day Sabbath (Saturday) is God's special day of worship (Genesis 2:1-3, Exodus 20:8-11);
Our works achieve the way to heaven.	The way to heaven is through faith in Jesus Christ (Ephesians 2:7-9).

The locusts not being able to harm vegetation:

In AD633, Abubeker, Mohammed's successor, sent out a circular letter to the Arabian tribes informing them of his intention to conquer Syria. He addressed the tribes as follows:

"When you fight the battles of the Lord, acquit yourselves like men, without turning your backs; but let not your victory be stained with the blood of women or children. Destroy no palm-trees, nor burn any fields of corn. Cut down no fruit-trees, nor do any mischief to cattle, only such as you kill to eat." ('Decline and fall of the Roman Empire', Edward Gibbon, volume 5, chapter 51, pages 442, 443)

Only harm those who do not have the seal of God:

Remember, those who have the seal of God on their foreheads are the ones who keep God's commandments as a result of being in a love relationship with Him.

"In the early centuries of the Christian era, the Church of the East sometimes called the Assyrian church, sometimes the Nestorian church (who were observers of the true Sabbath) very effectively spread throughout Asia and the East, but remained separate from the church in the West, especially the apostasy.

"These true Christians became the teachers of the Saracens, and were responsible for establishing an educational system in Syria, Mesopotamia, Turkistan, Tibet, China, India, Ceylon and others.

"The Arabs, like the Persians, were very partial to the Assyrian Christians, because they found it necessary in the early days of their power, to lean upon the splendid schools which the church had developed. Medicine made great progress in the hands of the Church of the East. The Arabian court and its extended administrations employed its members as secretaries and imperial representatives. . . Assyrian Christians suffered comparatively little at the hands of the Moslems, but later much more at the hands of the Jesuits". ('Truth Triumphant', BG Wilkinson page 291)

Revelation 9:1-4 give a series of clues in the description of the beginning of the fall of the Eastern Roman Empire. These clues, when compared with other Bible texts, and with history, enable us to put forward the following summary:

The Persians, led by Chosroes II, began attacking the Eastern Roman Empire. However, they were overtaken by the Arabian tribes, led by Mohammed, who brought to prominence the deceiving and fanatical teachings of Islam. Although immensely powerful, the Muslim campaigns were constricted by God who protected His people from their attacks.

Revelation 9:5 - We are given more information on the Muslim attack on the Eastern Roman Empire. The Muslims would torture the people, rather than obliterate them. This torture is described as the sting of a scorpion when it strikes, causing agony. This time of torture would last for five prophetic months.

Once again, the calculation of prophetic time comes into play. There are 30 days in each prophetic month, and we are looking at 5 months. Therefore, 5 x 30 = 150 prophetic days. As we know, in prophetic time – one prophetic day equals one literal year. Therefore, 150 prophetic days equal 150 literal years. (We will come back to this period later).

In the Arab-Byzantine wars (7th to 11th centuries AD) the Muslims did not completely destroy the Eastern Roman Empire, but over the centuries they were responsible for the conquests of Roman Syria, North Africa, Egypt, Cyrenaica, Exarchate of Africa, attacks on Anatolia, sieges on Constantinople, and battles with Byzantine (Eastern Roman) holdings in Africa, Sicily and the East. (Wikipedia – Arab-Byzantine wars)

Revelation 9:6 – The people being attacked by the Arab tribes would seek death but would not find it, they would long to die, but death would elude them. This gives insight into the ferocity of the Arabs who, having taken on a new religion (Islam), saw themselves as fighting a holy war, sanctioned by God. And, in their holy zeal, inflicted great suffering on their enemies (the infidels).

Revelation 9:7-10 – The locusts viewed by John are now described in detail. As shown by the chart below, each element corresponds to the historical Muslim soldier:

Bible Description	Muslim Soldier
The locusts looked like horses prepared for battle	We have already identified the fighting locusts as the Arab tribes. They are described as looking like horses. Arabian horses are famous worldwide, and were extensively used as war horses.

Bible Description	Muslim Soldier
They wore something like golden crowns on their heads.	Arabs of this time were distinguished by the richly embroidered turbans worn by their men.
Their faces resembled human faces.	This army, although described as locusts, were actual human beings.
Their hair was like women's hair.	Arab men wore their hair long.
They had lion's teeth.	This is a fitting symbol of the Arabs' ferocity, fearlessness, and strength in devouring their enemies.
They had breastplates of iron.	Arab soldiers wore an iron breastplate called a cuirass.
The sound of their wings was like the thundering of many horses and chariots rushing into battle.	This is powerful imagery of the Arabian cavalry thundering into battle. The Arabs were famous for their army of horses and chariots.
They had tails with stingers, like scorpions.	As seen in Isaiah 9:14,15, tails are symbolic of deceiving prophets, and the Arabs going into battle were led by Mohammed, a deceiving prophet who advocated mass torture.
Their tails had power to torment people for five months.	The Muslim armies would not totally destroy the Eastern Roman Empire, but would torment people, as instructed by the deceiving teachings of their false prophet, for five prophetic months (150 literal years).

Revelation 9:11 – We are told that the Muslim attackers had a king over them who is the angel of the Abyss, whose name in Hebrew is Abaddon, and in Greek Apollyon, which means Destroyer.

There are different schools of thought as to the starting point of the 150 years of Muslim torture, however it is believed this time period is linked to the king with the name 'Destroyer'. Destroyer cannot be a single king because of the length of his rule. It seems likely therefore that we are looking for a Muslim ruling empire that reigned for 150 years during the conquest of the Eastern Roman Empire.

The Muslim empire that fought against the Roman Eastern Empire for 150 years was the Ottoman Empire.

Here is a quote from 'Decline and Fall of the Roman Empire', Edward Gibbon, volume 7, chapter 64, page 25:

"It was on the twenty-seventh of July, in the year twelve hundred and ninety-nine of the Christian era, that Othman first invaded the territory of Nicomedia."

If the Ottoman Empire is the king named Destroyer referred to in Revelation 9:11, that would torment the people of the Eastern Roman Empire for 150 years, and, that period began on 27 July 1299, then there should be a significant event 150 years later to mark the end of the torment.

According to most historians, 154 years later on 29 May 1453, Constantinople, the capital of the Byzantine (Eastern Roman) Empire, was overtaken by the Turkish Ottoman Empire, which effectively put an end to the supreme 1,000 year rule of the Eastern Roman Empire. We will look at an alternative explanation of the 150 year period a little later.

Revelation 9:12 – At the close of Revelation 8 we were told that the final three trumpet blasts would hail three woes to the inhabitants of the earth. The Fifth Trumpet was the first woe. Now we will look at the second woe.

The Sixth Trumpet (Revelation 9:13-21)

Revelation 9:13 – As the Sixth Trumpet is sounded, we hear a voice coming from the four horns of the golden altar positioned before God.

We have already seen in Revelation 8:3 that the person ministering before the altar in the heavenly sanctuary is Jesus, our High Priest. He is still stationed before the golden altar with horns, that is the Altar of Incense (see Leviticus 16:17,18). This altar is in the Holy Place and therefore Jesus has not yet moved into the Most Holy Place. It follows, then, that the events of the Sixth Trumpet take place before 22 October 1844, when Jesus entered the Most Holy Place, and the Investigative Judgement began. (For an explanation of the sanctuary service and the move of Jesus from the Holy Place to the Most Holy Place in the heavenly sanctuary, please see the companion to this book 'An Idiot's Guide to the Book of Daniel', chapters 8:14 and 9).

Revelation 9:14-15 – The voice from the heavenly altar orders that the four destroying angels, presently bound at the river Euphrates, be loosed. The work of these angels has been reserved for *"this very hour, and day and month and year"*. Now they are released to kill a third of humankind.

We have seen four destroying angels before, in Revelation 7:1. However, the destructive power of the angels of the Sixth Trumpet does not threaten the whole earth. It originates from the area of the River Euphrates, and can only kill one-third of mankind.

Once again, we are given a prophetic time period for this killing spree – one hour, one day, one month and one year.

Remember, the calculation of prophetic time is governed by the Biblical day/year principle - one prophetic day equals one literal year (see Numbers 14:34, Ezekiel 4:6):

Our prophetic time period is: 1 hour, 1 day, 1 month, 1 year.

(The ancient Jewish/Hebrew calendar, known as the Biblical Lunar Calendar [BLC], has twelve 30 day months equalling 360 days).

A prophetic year = 360 prophetic days = 360 literal years

A prophetic month = 30 prophetic days = 30 literal years.

A prophetic day = 1 literal year.

A prophetic hour = 1/24 of a prophetic day = 1/24 of a literal year (360 literal days) = 15 literal days.

Total literal time period = 391 years, 15 days.

(We will come back to this time period.)

In Revelation 9:5 (under the Fifth Trumpet) the attacking Arabian tribes were allowed to torture the Eastern Roman Empire. Under the Sixth Trumpet the destroying power, now the Turkish Ottoman Empire (symbolised as the four destroying angels), is told to kill one-third of humanity. We have come across this killing of 'a third' before. In Revelation 8, when viewing the destruction of the Western Roman Empire, we were told that a third of everything would be destroyed. This refers to the west section of the empire being destroyed, not the whole Roman Empire. Similarly, in Revelation 9, when dealing with the Eastern Roman (or Byzantine) Empire, we are dealing with the east section of the Roman Empire, and so once again we are told that a third of mankind will be killed.

At this stage, after the torturing of the Eastern Roman Empire by the Arabs, and then the Ottoman Empire for 150 years, we are told it will finally be destroyed by the power originating from the area of the river Euphrates. It was the Ottoman Empire, a multi-national force dominated by the Turks, that came from the region of the Euphrates.

Revelation 9:16 - The destroying army would be vast. The cavalry alone would number 200 million.

Quotation from Decline and Fall of the Roman Empire:

"The myriads of Turkish horses overspread a frontier of six hundred miles from Taurus to Arzeroum, and the blood of one hundred and thirty thousand Christians was a grateful sacrifice to the Arabian prophet." ('Decline and Fall of the Roman Empire', Edward Gibbon, volume 6, chapter 42, page 245)

Revelation 9:17 - We see a description of the Turkish troops. The cavalry had breastplates of red, blue and yellow.

Quotation from 'Horae Apocalypticae', E B Elliott - chapter 7, page 508:

"From their first appearance the Ottomans have affected to wear warlike apparel of scarlet, blue and yellow: a descriptive trait the more marked from its contrast to the military appearance of Greeks, Franks or Saracens (Arabs) who were contemporary."

Revelation 9:17 - The horses' heads are like the heads of lions. This surely symbolises the ferocity of this army.

And, out of their mouths come fire, smoke and sulphur. The Turkish Ottoman Empire was known for its use of gunpowder fired by canons in battle. The Turkish army led by Mohammed II overthrew the city of Constantinople using canons.

Quotation from 'Decline and Fall of the Roman Empire', Edward Gibbon, volume 7, chapter 68, pages 176-202:

"There were many mechanical weapons used by Mahomet [Mohammed] II, that were pointed at the walls of Constantinople, fourteen batteries thundered at once on the most accessible places; and of one of these it is ambiguously expressed that it was mounted with one hundred and thirty guns, or that it discharged one hundred and thirty bullets . . . mechanical engines for casting

stones and darts; the bullet and the battering-ram were directed against the same walls.

"But this was not the most powerful of his weapons. A founder of canon (Urban by name), a Dane or Hungarian, who had been almost starved in the Greek service, deserted to the Moslems, and was liberally entertained by the Turkish sultan. Mahomet [Mohammed] was satisfied with the answer to his first question, which he eagerly pressed on the artist. Am I able to cast a canon capable of throwing a stone or ball of sufficient size to batter the walls of Constantinople? . . . a foundry was established at Hadrianople: the metal was prepared; and, at the end of three months, Urban produced a piece of brass ordnance of stupendous and almost incredible magnitude; a measure of twelve palms was assigned to the bore; and the stone bullet weighed about six hundred pounds (approx. 273 kgs).

"They fired the canon the next day, and the explosion was felt or heard for 100 furlongs. By the force of the gunpowder, the ball was driven for over a mile. On impact, it drove itself into the ground the depth of a fathom. It took them nearly 2 months to transport it to Constantinople.

"The great canon could be loaded and fired no more than seven times in one day. The heated metal unfortunately burst; several workmen were destroyed; and the skill of an artist was admired who bethought himself of preventing the danger and the accident, by pouring oil, after each explosion, into the mouth of the canon.

"Finally a breach was made in the wall, it was thus, after a siege of fifty-three days (this would bring the date to May 29 of 1453), that Constantinople, which had defied the power of Chosroes, the Chagan, and the caliphs, was irretrievably subdued by the arms of Mahomet [Mohammed] the Second."

Revelation 9:18 – Again, we are told that a third of mankind is killed. Specifically, they are killed by the fire, smoke and sulphur fired from the canons.

Revelation 9:19 - The Turks have horses that issue fire and brimstone or sulphur out of their mouths, and tails like snakes with heads that inflict injury. These are no ordinary horses of course. Their mouths that issue fire and brimstone appear to be their canon weaponry. The tails, which are like snakes with heads that inflict injury, could once again be the injury inflicted by their lying prophet, Mohammed. Moreover, just as Satan used the serpent to beguile Eve and bring sin into the world (see Genesis 3:1-6), it is clear who is influencing the lying prophet and where his lies come from.

Earlier, we calculated the prophetic time period of 'one hour, one day, one month and one year' to equal 391 years and 15 days of the destroying force of the Turkish Ottomans.

At the close of the Fifth Trumpet we learned that most historians agree that the 150 years of torture came to an end on 29 May 1453 with the fall of Constantinople. And, as history bears out, the 391 years and 15 days of killing followed the close of the 150 years of torture. If we add 391 years and 15 days to May 1453 this takes us to June 1844. As we have already seen, 1844 is an extremely important year for the church of God. (We will look at this in detail in Revelation chapter ten.)

Uriah Smith, in his book, 'Daniel and the Revelation' gives an alternative view. He states that the 150 years of the torture of the Eastern Roman Empire came to an end on 27 July 1449. (not 29 May 1453). If we add 391 years and 15 days to 27 July 1449, we come to the date 11 August 1840.

Quotation from 'Daniel and the Revelation' – Uriah Smith:

"Mehemet Ali, Pasha of Egypt, which was a vassal of the Sultan, decided to revolt and claim himself to be independent sovereign of Egypt, Arabia and Syria. He no longer was going to pay tribute to the Porte. This was in 1838.

"In 1839 hostilities again commenced, and were prosecuted, until, in a general battle between the armies of the Sultan and Mehemet, the Sultan's army was entirely cut up and destroyed, that, when hostilities commenced in August, he had only two first-rates and three frigates, as the sad remains of the once powerful Turkish fleet. This fleet Mehemet positively refused to give up and return to the Sultan, and declared, if the powers attempted to take it from him he would burn it.

"In this posture affairs stood, when, in 1840, England, Russia, Austria and Prussia (Germany) interposed, and determined on settlement of the difficulty, for it was evident, if left alone, Mehemet would soon become master of the Sultan's throne.

"The sultan accepted this intervention of the great powers, and thus made a voluntary surrender of the question into their hands. A conference of these powers was held in London, the Sheik Effendi Bey Likgis being present as Ottoman plenipotentiary. An ultimatum was drawn up to be presented to the pasha of Egypt, whereby the sultan was to offer him the hereditary government of Egypt, and all that part of Syria extending from the Gulf of Suez to the Lake of Tiberias together with the province of Acre, for life; he on his part to evacuate all other parts of the sultan's dominions then occupied by him, and to return the Ottoman fleet. In case he refused this offer from the sultan, the four powers were to take the matter into their own hands, and use such other means to bring him to terms as they should see fit.

"It is apparent that just as soon as this ultimatum should be put by the sultan into the hands of Mehemet Ali, the matter would be forever beyond the control of the former, and the disposal of his affairs would, from that moment, be in

the hands of foreign powers. The sultan despatched Rifat Bey on a government steamer to Alexandria, to communicate the ultimatum to the pasha. It was put into his hands, and by him taken in charge, on the eleventh day of August, 1840! (A letter of a correspondent of the London Morning Chronicle, of September 18, 1840, dated, Constantinople, August 27th, 1840 and also Constantinople August 12th, 1840, confirms this date) On the same day, a note was addressed by the sultan to the ambassadors of the four powers, inquiring what plan was to be adopted in case the pasha should refuse to comply with the terms of the ultimatum, to which they made answer that provision had been made, and there was no necessity of his alarming himself about any contingency that might arise . . . where was the sultan's independence? — GONE!" (Daniel and the Revelation', Uriah Smith, pages 486, 487)

The Ottoman Empire lost its independence on the 11 August 1840, with a bloodless take-over by the four powers, England, Russia, Prussia, and Austria. This marks the end of the 391 years and 15 days of destructive power of the Ottoman Empire.

Revelation 9:20-21 - Although the Eastern Roman Empire was completely decimated by the Ottoman Empire, we are told that some people remained. These people would not repent of the work they were engaged in. They would not stop worshiping demons; making idols of gold, silver, bronze, stone and wood; useless and lifeless idols. Nor would they repent of their murders, magic arts, sexual immorality, nor their thefts. Despite the fall of the Roman Empire, the apostate church, comprised of people who defy the worship of the true God, would remain, performing their devilish acts. This does not bode well for God's people.

We have one trumpet to go, and we have already been warned the Seventh Trumpet will be a tale of woe.

However, before we get to the final trumpet, we are given a break in proceedings as we take a look at two points in history concerning the fate of God's church.

Revelation Chapter Ten

THE LITTLE SCROLL

Based on Revelation 10:1-11

We have arrived at a hiatus in our study of the Seven Trumpets. This is much like the interruption of the Seven Seals in Revelation chapter six.

The Seventh Trumpet is the third promised 'woe', and portrays the end of time, and the heralding of God's final judgements. However, before we reach there, John is shown two visions of important events affecting God's church.

Revelation 10:1 – John sees a mighty being, whom he describes as an angel, coming down from heaven. This being is robed in a cloud, with a rainbow above His head. His face is like the sun, and His legs are like fiery pillars.

Although John describes Him as an angel, this being bears a striking resemblance to descriptions of Jesus in other Bible texts, as follows:

The Being of Revelation 10	Characteristics of Jesus
Robed in a cloud	He comes with clouds (Revelation 1:7)
A rainbow above His head	A rainbow encircles the throne of God (Revelation 4:3)
His face is like the sun	His face is like the sun shining in all its brilliance (Revelation 1:16)
His legs are like fiery pillars	His feet are like bronze glowing in a furnace (Revelation 1:15)

The Being is Jesus.

Revelation 10:2 – John sees Jesus holding a little scroll, and notes that the scroll is open. This is not the scroll with the Seven Seals in Revelation 5 and 6: this is a 'little' scroll. The fact that it is little seems significant. Perhaps it is little because it is part of a larger book. Also, it is open, implying that at one time it may have been closed.

There is a book in the Bible that was instructed to be closed until a certain time. This is the book of Daniel. In Daniel 12:4 the angel, interpreting Daniel's visions, says to him, *"But you, Daniel, roll up and seal the words of the scroll until the time of the end. Many will go here and there to increase knowledge."*

Now, in Revelation 10, we see the little scroll, once instructed to be closed, is open, confirmation that John is viewing the time of the end, when the visions of Daniel will be understood and preached.

Jesus plants His right foot on the sea, and His left foot on the land. Apparently, the book of Daniel is a message for the whole earth, both the densely populated and sparsely populated regions. It is for the people of earth to understand.

Revelation 10:3 – Jesus gives a loud shout; like the roar of a lion. What He is about to say is important and must be heard, for it is announced with a lion's roar; Jesus is trying to get our attention. As Jesus shouts, John hears the voices of the seven thunders.

When God speaks it can sound like thunder. At Jesus' baptism, the voice of God was heard from heaven, and some people recognised it as a voice, while others said it thundered (see John 12:28-30). Therefore, when John hears a voice of seven thunders (the number of perfection), we can safely assume this is the voice of God.

Revelation 10:4 – John hears what the seven thunders say, and is about to write it down, but is instructed to seal up what was said, and not write it.

Therefore, we will never know what the seven thunders said - but we can speculate.

As John's vision is set at the end of earth's history, perhaps what was revealed by the seven thunders is information God has purposely kept from human beings, such as the date of Jesus' second coming. In Matthew 24:36,42 Jesus says, *"But about that day or hour no-one knows . . . only the Father". "Therefore keep watch, because you do not know on what day your Lord will come."* Clearly, God does not reveal the date of the Second Coming. The event might be far in our future, which could discourage those expecting to see it in their time. Equally, human beings have a tendency to wait until the last minute before preparing for a known event. It is God's will that all be saved. Therefore, in every age, the answer to the question 'When will Jesus come again?' is 'Soon' (see Revelation 22:20), which keeps us in a state of readiness. If it is the case that the date was announced by the seven thunders, little wonder John was instructed not to write it down. It would not benefit humanity to know this. Whatever the seven thunders said is not for us to hear at this time.

As we will find later in this chapter, the fact that God has not revealed the date of the Second Coming does not prevent people from seeking this information.

Revelation 10:5-6 – Jesus then raises His right hand to heaven, and swears by Him who lives forever and ever, the Creator of the heavens, the earth, the seas and all the inhabitants of them.

In John 1:1-3, we are told Jesus is the Creator (along with the other persons of the Godhead). So actually, Jesus is swearing by Himself, and He has done this before. Hebrews 6:13 says *"When God made His promise to Abraham, since there was no-one greater for Him to swear by, He swore by Himself."* In Revelation, Jesus swears by Himself, and we can rest assured that a promise made by God on His own surety will certainly be fulfilled. What does He promise? *"There will be no more delay!"* Jesus is confirming that when the

110

little scroll is opened the world will have reached the time of the end, His coming will be soon.

The King James Version of the Bible translates the words of Jesus in Revelation 10:6 as, *"That there should be time no longer."* Some interpret this phrase to mean that, as the book of Daniel is the little scroll being referred to, and which contains the longest time prophecy in the Bible ending in 1844, the phrase *"That there should be time no longer"* indicates there will be no time prophecies after 1844. Consequently, 1844 is the final date in Bible prophecy. After that date, Jesus could come at any time. (For an explanation of this prophecy, called the 2,300 days prophecy, please see the companion book 'An Idiot's Guide to the Book of Daniel' chapter 9).

Revelation 10:7 – Jesus goes on to say, in the days when the Seventh Trumpet is about to be blown, the mystery of God will be accomplished, just as He announced to His servants the prophets.

As the seventh and last trumpet announces the coming of Jesus, He is confirming that this vision is for the last days, just before the Seventh Trumpet sounds. God is about to wrap everything up. What is the mystery of God that will be accomplished? In Colossians 1:27 Paul says, *"To them God has chosen to make known among the Gentiles the glorious riches of this mystery, which is Christ in you, the hope of glory."* The mystery of God is the gospel of salvation; the good news that Jesus came to planet earth in human form, lived, died for our sins, and rose from the dead. And, that through our acceptance of His sacrifice, we gain eternal life. This is indeed a mystery. When the mystery is revealed to the whole world, giving everyone the chance to be saved, then Jesus will come (see Matthew 24:14). The Biblical prophets knew of this mystery and proclaimed it. Every book in the Bible makes known the mystery of God working on mankind in order to save us.

Revelation 10:8-10 – John hears a voice from heaven instructing him to take the scroll from the hand of Jesus. This is further confirmation that this little scroll is not the same one we encountered in Revelation chapter five. That scroll could not be opened by anyone except Jesus. This one is already open, and is for humankind; John was to take it from the hand of Jesus.

John obeys the command and takes the scroll, whereupon Jesus instructs him to eat it. Jesus tells him, it will be as sweet as honey in his mouth but bitter in his stomach. We do not have to wait long for the fulfilment of this prophecy. John eats the book and indeed it is as sweet as honey in his mouth, but then gives him a painful stomach ache.

Prophets in vision have been instructed to eat books before. Jeremiah describes his joyous experience of eating God's words (see Jeremiah 15:16), and Ezekiel was told to eat a scroll in order to give a *"sweet as honey"* message to the people (see Ezekiel 3:1-3). It is clear, when God has a message for the people of earth, the messenger must fully take it in, learn it, digest it, and make it part of their being in order to teach it. To God's messengers, His words are sweet, but with the little scroll in Revelation 10, although the message was sweet in the mouth, it had a very bitter after taste.

Revelation 10:11 – John is suffering physical pain, but Jesus comforts him with the words *"You must prophesy again about peoples, nations, languages and kings."* Thus, although the message given would bring severe pain to the messengers, Jesus exhorts them not to be discouraged and stop; they must continue proclaiming to the world.

What does this prophecy mean?

There was a time in history when the book of Daniel became the focus of Christians worldwide. This corresponds with the Philadelphian era already discussed in Chapter Three. New truths were being learned from the ancient book previously viewed as closed. The prophecies of Daniel were now open, plain and understandable.

In the USA, during the early 1800s, a Baptist American Farmer, called William Miller, felt divinely led to study the prophecies of Daniel. This was a book about peoples, nations, languages and kings, beginning with Babylon's king Nebuchadnezzar in 605BC, and ending with the second coming of Jesus. Miller came to the 2,300 days prophecy (See Daniel 8:14, 9:20-27) and deciphered the prophecy's time lines. (For a full explanation of the 2,300 days prophecy, please see the companion book 'An Idiot's Guide to the Book of Daniel', chapter 9).

It was now 1819, and Miller believed the prophecy was pointing to the coming of Jesus, and the end of the world, and that the actual date of this event was given as 22 October 1844.

Miller was not alone in reaching this conclusion. Around the same time, European Bible scholars, who knew nothing about Miller's findings, were also studying the book of Daniel and preaching the same message throughout Europe. William Miller became an evangelist, and together with others, spread the news throughout the USA. The message that the Second Advent would take place in 1844 quickly became a worldwide movement attracting hundreds of thousands of believers from various denominations, who took to calling themselves 'Adventists'; for, despite their doctrinal differences they were united in their belief in the second coming of Jesus.

As 1844 drew near, the Adventists closed their businesses, stopped tending their farms, left their places of work and became evangelists. And finally, in October 1844 the Adventists congregated in groups ready to meet Jesus. 22 October dawned, and they waited in great anticipation, but the day passed and Jesus did not appear. It was a devastating disappointment, and the event is now known as 'the Great Disappointment'. As Revelation 10:10 prophesied, the message that Jesus would come, which was so sweet in the mouths of the Adventists who believed it and preached it to the nations, turned sour, when Jesus did not appear. The believers had to return to their homes, their wasted

113

farms, unbelieving neighbours, and taunting onlookers. A great disappointment indeed.

Many Adventists lost their faith. Their confidence in the movement was gone. They felt humiliated and let down, and could not comprehend why God had allowed them to undergo this demeaning experience. Some went back to their original churches, and many joined in ridiculing their former Adventist brethren.

However, out of estimated 300,000 Adventists, there was a small group, around fifty in number, who did not lose hope. They were encouraged by Revelation 10:11 where John was instructed that after the disappointment *"you must prophesy again before many peoples, and nations, and tongues, and kings."* (KJV). They reasoned that God could not be wrong, so they must be in error.

Some Adventists continued to set new dates for the Second Coming, but the fifty went back to their Bibles to look again at the prophecy in Daniel. They had faith that God had not forsaken them, and so prayed for the true interpretation, believing there was something for them to learn from this experience. They rechecked the time line of the 2,300 days prophecy and found it to be sound. Therefore, the only thing they could have misunderstood was the cleansing of the sanctuary referred to in Daniel 8:14, which they had assumed was the end of the world.

As they studied, they compared the prophecy with the book of Hebrews, and learned the sanctuary to be cleansed was not the earth, but the heavenly temple sanctuary; where Jesus is now presiding as our High Priest (see Hebrews 8:1,2). Moreover, just as the earthly wilderness sanctuary was cleansed every year on the Day of Atonement (see Leviticus 16), there was a time set for the cleansing of the heavenly sanctuary. This cleansing would rid the sanctuary of the sins of God's people, just as on the earthly Day of

Atonement. Therefore, the earthly event was a type of the true heavenly ceremony, which would begin on 22 October 1844, and would continue until just before Jesus' coming. It was then clear that, instead of the earth being destroyed, this was the date that Jesus, our High Priest, entered the Most Holy Place in the heavenly sanctuary to stand before the throne of God and plead His blood for all those who truly follow Him.

With this knowledge came the realisation that the cleansing of the heavenly sanctuary was the investigation of the record books of God's professed followers (see Daniel 7:9,10). If the examination of their books shows their sins are confessed and so covered with the blood of Jesus, then their names are retained in the Book of Life, and they are confirmed as God's rightful heirs. As a result, their sins are placed on the true culprit, and originator of sin - the devil. In this way, the sanctuary is cleansed of their sins.

Those professed Christians whose sins remain unconfessed, when their life books are examined, will have their names expunged from the Book of Life. (We will examine their fate in Revelation chapter twenty.)

The fifty finally understood the reason for the Great Disappointment. God was preparing an end time church that trusted and served Him through the worst of experiences; a mature people who know God for who He really is, and whose faith could not be shaken. That is why Jesus said in Revelation 10:11, "*you must prophesy again*". For these people would be given a work to do.

In addition, they realised that as soon as the Investigative Judgement was concluded Jesus would come (see Daniel 12:1-3). They believed that, as the end time church, God had given them an urgent end time message to preach to "*peoples, and nations, and tongues, and kings.*" And, they found the message in Revelation 14:6-12, which we now call 'The Three Angels' Messages'. This is the end time message for the end time people, and it is preached only by the end time church. (We will look at this message in Chapter Fourteen).

The small group of Adventists, aged mainly in their teens and early twenties, formed a church, and took their lead directly from their study of the Bible. A few years after their formation they realised that the seventh-day Sabbath instituted by God to commemorate creation (see Genesis 2:1-3), and confirmed in the Ten Commandments (see Exodus 20:8-11), has never been changed by God; and they began to observe it. It was at this time (1863) that they renamed themselves Seventh-day Adventists. They were keepers of the seventh-day Sabbath who still believed in the second coming of Jesus, but understood that no date for the event was given in the Bible.

The Seventh-day Adventist church is the only denomination that preaches the 2,300 days prophecy. The church believes the Great Disappointment was the means used by God to specifically set up an end time church to preach The Three Angels' Messages to the world in order to prepare it for the second coming of Christ. Seventh-day Adventists do not claim to know the date of the Second Coming, but they do believe their God-given mission is an urgent one.

Revelation Chapter Eleven

THE TWO WITNESSES

Based on Revelation 11:1-19

Revelation 11 is the second vision given to John that interrupts the Seven Trumpets, and like Revelation 10, this vision is historically positioned between the events of the Sixth Trumpet (the destruction of the Eastern Roman Empire), and the Second Coming; when the Seventh Trumpet will sound. However, the era of Revelation 11 actually comes before the events of Revelation chapter ten (the great Advent Awakening).

At first glance, this seems a strange way of recording historical events, but Revelation 10 depicts how people were led to the study of the Word of God; to treasure the Word and hold fast to it amidst derision and ridicule. Whereas, as we shall see, Revelation 11 shows a time before the Advent Awakening, when the Bible was hated and held in contempt. These two chapters remind us that time's pendulum often swings from one extreme to the other; a time of spiritual chaos can lead to a time of devout worship, and in-depth study of the Word of God.

Revelation 11:1 - John is shown a vision in which he must participate. He is given a measuring rod and asked to measure the temple of God. Whenever we have seen the temple in Revelation, it has always been the temple in heaven. Therefore, we can assume this is also the case here.

Why would John be asked to measure the temple in heaven? In Zechariah 2:1,2, Zechariah sees a vision of an angel with a measuring line sent to measure the city of Jerusalem soon to be rebuilt. This vision was given as reassurance to Zechariah that the rebuilding of Jerusalem would indeed take place.

Therefore, John's task of measuring the temple of God, its altar, and its worshipers, appears to be reassurance that the temple in heaven and Jesus' ministry there, are real. We can believe Jesus is our High Priest: He is mediating on our behalf before the altar. The worshipers are obviously God's people, symbolically they are shown as being in God's temple.

In Revelation 21, John will witness the measuring of a city; once again as reassurance of its existence.

Revelation 11:2 - John is specifically told not to measure the outer court of the temple because it has been given to the Gentiles who will trample on the holy city for 42 months.

The apostle Paul speaks of the partition wall that existed in the Jerusalem temple in his day, separating the Jews from the Gentiles (see Ephesians 2:11-14). In John's vision, the worshipers of God are within the temple, whilst the Gentiles, symbolic of those who do not worship God, are relegated to the outer court. They are not allowed to enter the measured area because they are clearly not God's people; for these symbolic Gentiles are those who will trample on the holy city for 42 months. It is clear, the pretenders in the outer court purport to be of the household of faith, but their behaviour belies their claim.

The 42 month period is, of course, symbolic time, and so we must use the prophetic time formula of one prophetic day equals one literal year (see Ezekiel 4:6). As we already know, the ancient Jewish calendar (or BLC) designates 30 days to each month. Therefore, 42 prophetic months equal 1,260 prophetic days (42 x 30). Then we apply the prophetic time formula which gives us 1,260 literal years.

1,260 years of religious persecution is a famous time period which historians call 'The Dark Ages'. It began in AD538 and ended in 1798. During this time

Papal Rome ruled Europe in a reign of religious oppression; persecuting all who did not bow to its will, including those who followed the Bible instead of the dictates of the Papacy. Thus, in Revelation 11, the symbolic Gentiles, or non-worshipers, are identified as Papal Rome. We come across this period of persecution, the 1,260 years, repeatedly in Revelation.

Revelation 11:3 – Here is our introduction to the Two Witnesses. They are appointed by God, and will prophecy during the 1,260 year period dressed in sackcloth; the ancient garment of mourning. These witnesses are eyewitnesses of the horrific martyrdoms of the Dark Ages. Who are these witnesses? They cannot be actual individuals as they span the 1,260 year period.

Revelation 11:4 – We are told the Two Witnesses are the two olive trees, and the two lampstands, and they stand before the Lord of the earth. The prophet Zechariah was also given a vision of the olive trees and lampstands (see Zechariah 4:1-6). He was told they are symbolic of the work of the Holy Spirit.

As John sees the same symbols, we can deduce they have the same meaning: the Two Witnesses are carrying out the work of the Holy Spirit. Moreover, it must be significant that there are two of them.

Revelation 11:5-6 – We are given more characteristics of the witnesses to enable us to identify them. Let us compare their characteristics with features of the Bible:

The Two Witnesses	Bible Features
There are two of them.	The Bible has an Old and New Testament.
The Two Witnesses prophesy.	The Bible holds the prophecies of God.

The Two Witnesses	Bible Features
They are described as oil and light and carry out the work of the Holy Spirit.	Psalm 119:105 describes the Bible as a lamp giving light. Zechariah 4:1-6 shows lamps fuelled by oil as the work of the Holy Spirit, which fuels the Word of God.
Fire comes out of the mouths of the Witnesses to devour their enemies.	2 Kings 1:10,12 describe how fire fell from heaven to devour God's enemies.
The Witnesses have the power to shut up heaven so that it will not rain.	In 1 Kings 17:1, Elijah told King Ahab it would not rain for 3.1/2 years; and his prophecy came true.
The Witnesses have power to turn the waters into blood, and to strike the earth with every kind of plague.	Exodus 7-11 and Revelation 16 both describe God's plagues unleashed on the earth, including the turning of waters into blood.

The above comparisons give ample evidence that the Two Witnesses are in fact the Bible (made up of the Old and New Testaments), which, under the guidance of the Holy Spirit, continued to be the means of spreading the gospel, despite the widespread religious persecution of the Dark Ages.

Here are some quotations which show the attitude and actions of the Roman Catholic Church during the Dark Ages:

"The Roman Emperor, Justinian . . . enriched himself with the property of all 'heretics' – that is, non-Catholics; published edicts in 538AD compelling all to join the Catholic church in 90 days or leave the empire and have all their goods confiscated." ('History of the Christian Church From its Establishment by Christ to AD 1871', N Summerbell, pages 310-311.)

"The Papacy regarded the Bible as the source of all heresy and that it made good heretics and thus the reading of it was prohibited and condemned." ('The History of Protestantism', JA Wylie, volume 1, page 45)

"The decree of Toulouse 1229AD [in France] which established the 'Tribunal of the Inquisition' against all readers of the Bible in the common tongue . . . was an edict of fire, bloodshed and devastation . . . it ordained the entire destruction of houses, the humblest places of the concealment and even the subterranean retreats of men convicted of possessing the scriptures; that they should be pursued to the forest and caves of the earth, and that even those who harboured them should be severely punished. As a result, the Bible was everywhere prohibited; it was vanished, as it were, underground; it descended into the tomb. These decrees were followed for five hundred years by innumerable punishments, in which the blood of the saints flowed like water." ('The Canon of the Holy Scriptures', L Gaussen, Part 2, Book 2, Chapter 7, sec 2, prop. 642 paragraph 2)

Revelation 11:7 – The above quotations confirm that during the 1,260 years, the Roman Catholic Church attacked the Bible, and killed those who adhered to its teachings. But now we are told that at the end of this period of persecution, when the Two Witnesses have finished their testimony, a beast comes up out of the Abyss to attack, overpower and kill them.

We know that in prophecy, a beast represents a power or kingdom (see Daniel 7:23). Towards the end of the Dark Ages there was a country that initiated a brutal attack on the Word of God. Significantly, this power comes up out of the Abyss, or Bottomless Pit to attack God's Word. This surely is not a power from God, but rather of satanic origin.

Before we identify this beast, we are given more details of its ungodly behaviour.

Revelation 11:8-10 – The beast lays the bodies of the Two Witnesses in the public square of the great city, figuratively called Sodom and Egypt, where their Lord was crucified.

To identify the beast, we must look carefully at its characteristics:

- It is a prophetic beast, therefore it must be a power or kingdom;
- It is of satanic origin for it comes up out of the Bottomless Pit;
- It attacks and kills the Word of God – it aids and abets the Roman Catholic Church, which attacked the Bible throughout the Dark Ages. However, this beast goes further; it kills the Bible around the end of the time of persecution, 1798.

Furthermore:

- The beast lays the Bible in the public square of the great city figuratively called Sodom and Egypt. In the book of Genesis, the city of Sodom was known as a place of sexual deviancy, and in the book of Exodus, Egypt was known as a country that defied God.
- In this great city Jesus was crucified. Matthew 25:40 tells us that whatever is done to the followers of Jesus, He considers as being done to Him. So, this power would be involved in the killing of the followers of Jesus.
- The killing of the Bible would continue for three and a half years, observed by people from all other nations of the world.
- The people of the world would gloat over this ill-treatment of the Bible, because its teachings condemned them. They would send each other gifts in celebration.

Let us now look at the country of France, and its behaviour during the French Revolution (1789 – 1799). The causes of the Revolution stem from the injustices of the French system of governance over the poor. The peasants rose up to overthrow the monarchy, the ruling classes, and the political and social systems of the country. Moreover, as part of this violent and bloody action, they also sought to shake off the religious restraint of the Roman Catholic Church; the State religion at the time. The French Church had been heavily involved in the persecution and martyrdom of millions of Catholic dissenters, and now the ordinary people, kept under heavy oppression in every stratum of society, threw off all controls, and erupted into a bloodthirsty mob, using the guillotine daily to execute an estimated total of 25,000 people. The peasants targeted all those in positions of influence, including the religious leaders. They saw the Catholic Church as another oppressor, along with the monarchy, aristocracy, politicians, and the wealthy. All were to be brought down. And, as the Church had set itself up as the guardian of all things religious, everything relating to religion was thrown out.

The backdrop of the Revolution was the so-called Age of Reason (1570-1789) generally put forward as a time of enlightenment. This movement sought to replace God with the dictates of men. And so, without the moral guidance found in the teachings of the Bible, the stage was set for man to behave savagely, without decency or compassion.
(www.britannica.com.event/French-Revolution)
(Wikipedia – French Revolution Age of Reason)

Here are some quotations on the French Revolution:

"France manifested the same God-defying spirit that was seen in the kingdom of Egypt, Exodus 5:2, the king of the south. This then is a resurrection of the God-defying spirit of atheism direct from a satanic origin."

(www.revelationbibleprophecy.org/revelation11)

"The [French] Convention dressed an ass . . . loaded it with the symbols of Christianity and tied the Old and New Testaments to its tail. It was then led in a mock procession. . . . The crowd piled books of devotion into heaps and burned them to ashes, amid blasphemous shouts. . . . A prostitute was enthroned as 'Goddess of Reason . . ." ('Prophetic Faith of Our Fathers', LE Froom, volume 2, page 738)

"On November 26, 1793, the Convention, of which 17 bishops and some clergy were members, decreed the abolition of religion." ('The Age of Revolution', W.H. Hutton, page 156)

"In the Revolution the institution of marriage was made a mockery and great immorality took place, just like the licentious Sodom (Genesis 13:13; 19:4-11; Jude 7)" (www.revelationbibleprophecy.org/revelation11)

". . . in the scenes of the Revolution, Jesus Christ was declared to be an impostor, and the rallying cry of the French infidels was, 'Crush the Wretch', meaning Christ. Heaven-daring blasphemy and abominable wickedness went hand-in-hand, and the basest of men, the most abandoned monsters of cruelty and vice, were most highly exalted. In all this, supreme homage was paid to Satan, while Christ, in His characteristics of truth, purity, and unselfish love, was crucified."
(www.revelationbibleprophecy.org/revelation11)

Now we have identified the beast who comes up out of the Bottomless Pit as the country of France, let us look at how this nation treated the Bible during the French Revolution.

Revelation 11:8-10 – tell us, the bodies of the Two Witnesses, whom we have identified as the Bible, would be left dead in the streets for the world to gaze on for three and a half days, but it would not be buried. The inhabitants of the earth would gloat over them and send gifts to each other in celebration because the Bible had tormented them.

The three and a half days are, of course, prophetic time. We must use the day/year principle once again - one prophetic day equals one literal year (see Numbers 14:34, Ezekiel 4:6). Therefore, three and a half prophetic days equal three and a half literal years.

During the Revolution, in their efforts to abolish God and religion, the people of France gathered Bibles into great piles in the streets and set fire to them. The people sang, danced and made merry at these bonfire gatherings, congratulating themselves on having rid the nation of all godly behaviour. They now felt free to act devoid of conscience.

"With blasphemous boldness almost beyond belief, one of the priests of the new order said: 'God, if You exist, avenge Your injured name. I bid You defiance! You remain silent; You dare not launch Your thunders. Who after this will believe in Your existence?" ('Lacretelle, History', volume II, page 309; in 'History of Europe', Sir Archibald Alison, volume I, chapter 10)

"France stands apart in the world's history as the single state which, by the decree of her Legislative Assembly, pronounced there was no God, and of which the entire population of the capital, and a vast majority elsewhere, women as well as men, danced and sang with joy in accepting the announcement." ('Blackwood's Magazine', November 1870)

The nation sought to replace every biblical principle with man-made edicts, such as the seventh-day Sabbath instituted at creation (see Genesis 2:1-3).

". . . the weekly rest-day was blotted out, and every tenth day substituted, for mirth and profanity." ('Daniel and the Revelation', Uriah Smith, page 501)

Revelation 11:11-12 – After the three and a half year period the Bible would come to life again, stand on its feet, and thereby strike terror into everyone who saw it. A great voice from heaven would proclaim *"Come up here"* and the Two Witnesses were gathered up in a cloud to heaven while their enemies looked on.

The French government came to regret its actions, for, without the influence of Bible principle, and belief in God, the nation became ungovernable as men gave expression to every passion, inclination, emotion, and action, without consideration of moral duty.

The decree to suppress the Bible, passed by the French Assembly in 1793, was hastily repealed three and a half years later on 17 June 1797.

Moreover, from the end of the French Revolution in 1799, the promise that the Bible would be exalted in the sight of men has truly been fulfilled. For, as we have already seen, in Revelation 10, the Advent Awakening followed, with worldwide increased interest in the Bible, its prophecies, and the coming of Jesus.

Revelation 11:13 – We are told that at that very hour (referring to the time when the Two Witnesses were once again given life, that is, towards the end of the French Revolution), there was a severe earthquake and a tenth of the city collapsed. Seven thousand people were killed in the earthquake, and the survivors were terrified and gave glory to the God of heaven.

This verse tells of the great destruction that would come about by the end of the French Revolution. Not only would there be great loss of life but the nation would be ruined. Please see the following quotations:

"It was an earthquake in the political world." ('Reflections on the Revolution in France', Edmund Burke)

"It destroyed the landmarks of the world in which generations of men had passed their lives." (Cambridge Modern History)

The Revolution, rather than solving the injustices of the French system, caused more tyranny, death, destruction, and left the population in a state of trepidation.

The reference to 'a tenth of the city collapsing' could identify France as one of the ten kingdoms of Europe into which the Roman Empire was divided at its demise (see Daniel 7:23,24). And, if 'the city' is Babylon (the apostate church through the ages) which includes the Roman Catholic Church, (see Revelation 17:18), then the collapse of a tenth of the city may refer to the collapsed state of France after the Revolution.We are also told that seven thousand people were killed in the earthquake. Some Bible scholars look to the Greek translation here that may refer to seven thousand 'titles of men' rather than 'people'.

Here is a quotation describing the abolishment of titles, offices and orders during the Revolution:

"Hereditary nobility is forever abolished: in consequence the titles of prince, duke, count, marquis, viscount, vidame, baron, knight, messive, ecuyler, noble and all other similar titles, shall neither be taken by any one whomsoever nor given to anybody." ('Constitution and Selected Documents', FM Anderson, page 33)

The number 'seven thousand' is, no doubt, symbolic. As seven is the symbol of completeness, this could refer to the complete dissolution of the titled French ruling classes. To this day, the titles of the aristocracy have not been reinstated in France.

Verse 13 ends with the results of the Revolution. It says *"the survivors were terrified and gave glory to the God of heaven."*

Here is a quotation from 'Daniel and the Revelation':

"Their God-dishonouring and Heaven-defying work filled France with such scenes of blood, carnage, and horror, as made even the infidels themselves tremble, and stand aghast; and the 'remnant' that escaped the horrors of that hour 'gave glory to God' – not willingly, but the God of heaven caused this 'wrath of man to praise him,' by causing all the world to see that those who make war on heaven make graves for themselves; thus glory redounded to God by the very means that the wicked men ployed to tarnish that glory." ('Daniel and the Revelation', Uriah Smith, pages 504,505)

There is no doubt, the French Revolution is an object lesson to all generations, for it shows the fate of humankind when they turn their backs on God.

Now that we have examined the second hiatus in the Seven Trumpets, we can return to the original subject.

The Seventh Trumpet

Revelation 11:14 – Revelation 8:13 warns that the last three trumpets are three woes. Now we are told that with the Seventh Trumpet comes the last of the three woes.

Revelation 11:15 – The seventh angel blows his trumpet, and there are loud voices in heaven, which shout:

"The kingdom of the world has become the kingdom of our Lord and of His Messiah, and he will reign for ever and ever."

The Seventh Trumpet takes us forward in time. Here are the voices of angels in heaven proclaiming the time has come for God to bring an end to the system on earth. It is time for the Second Advent; Jesus will come, sweep away the kingdoms of the world and set up the kingdom of God on the earth.

Revelation 11:16-18 – This proclamation causes the twenty-four elders, whom we met in Revelation chapter four, who serve God in the heavenly temple and are therefore stationed around the throne of God, to fall down and worship God with a new song of praise:

"We give thanks to you Lord God Almighty,
the One who is and who was,
because you have taken your great power
and have begun to reign.
The nations were angry,
and your wrath has come.
The time has come for judging the dead,
and for rewarding your servants the prophets
and your people who revere your name,
both great and small –
and for destroying those who destroy the earth."

Their song welcomes the time when all the evil practised by men will cease. The Seven Trumpets have highlighted the anger of nations who strive with each other, causing war and destruction, but now it is time for the final wrath of God. He will judge the dead, in other words, those who have died will be judged for their deeds. Also, His faithful people will receive their reward (we will learn more about the judgement of the dead in Revelation chapter twenty). Included in the retribution God will bring on the earth, is the destruction of those who destroy the planet.

The manner in which we treat our planet does not go unnoticed by God. He sees the pollution, global warming and climate change, irresponsible industrial practices and waste disposal, engineered extinction of animal species; environmental abuse; all we do that destroys the beautiful globe on which we live. Those who continue to do such things will receive their deserved punishment.

Revelation 11:19 – John then once again sees God's temple in heaven, and it is open. He sees straight into the Most Holy Place where the Ark of the Covenant is situated. This scene indicates the Investigative Judgement that takes place in the Most Holy Place has been completed. And, as we know, once this judgement is over, Jesus will return to earth.

Then, there are flashes of lightning, rumblings, peals of thunder, an earthquake and a severe hailstorm; all the heavenly signs that herald the Second Coming.

To the people who worship God, this is good news, but to those who have not given their hearts to Jesus, this is indeed a time of woe, for they must face their fate. As we have already seen in Revelation chapter six under the Sixth Seal, they are the ones who will rather seek suicide than face the King of kings and Lord of lords. The Seventh Trumpet, therefore, heralds the woe of those unprepared for the Second Advent.

The Seven Trumpets have been sounded.

Footnote:

Three and a half years is certainly a significant Biblical time period. It reoccurs throughout the Bible, for example:

- 1 Kings 17 – God prevented rain from falling for three and a half years to punish king Ahab for his wicked leadership. God knew that without rain the land could not survive longer than three and half years before being irreversibly damaged. God was teaching Ahab that his rule was separating Israel from Him, and leading the whole nation to destruction.

- Jesus' ministry lasted three and a half years (AD27-AD31). This was the length of time sinful man could tolerate the sinless Messiah's ministry, before killing Him. Jesus came to reconcile mankind to God; to breach the separation caused by sin.

- Daniel 9 gives the explanation of the longest time prophecy in the Bible called the 2,300 Days. As part of the explanation, we are told in verse 27 that Jesus will confirm a covenant with many for one week (prophetic time which equals seven literal years), and that in the middle of the week, that is, after three and a half years of ministry, Jesus will put an end to the Jewish sacrificial system by His death (verse 26). Then, following the next three and a half years, which completes the seven year period, the time decreed for the Jews as God's chosen nation will come to an end (verse 24). Therefore, the period from the death of Jesus in AD31 to AD34 is the last three and a half years before the Jewish nation is separated from its special relationship with God. After that time, the disciples were instructed to take the gospel to the Gentiles. (For a full explanation of the 2,300 Days prophecy, please see the companion book 'An Idiot's Guide to the Book of Daniel', chapter 9).

- Daniel 7:25, 12:7, Revelation 12:14 – the three and a half prophetic years (1,260 literal years) of Papal religious persecution. This prophetic period given over to the anti-Christ (a time when the dominant Christian church separated itself from God) is a counterfeit of the real Christ's ministry (three and a half literal years), and shows that the result of the devil's ministry always leads to persecution, pain and death.

- Revelation 11:9,11 – The Two Witnesses (the Bible) die for three and a half years; a time when men tried to abolish God from their lives.

These examples, involving the time period three and a half years, highlight the consequences of separation from God. Genesis chapter one tells us we were made by God, in His image to live in harmony with Him. We live on a planet created by Him to be our home. We were appointed caretakers of the planet and everything on it, and we are responsible to God, the Owner of it all. Therefore, any attempt to separate ourselves from Him goes against our purpose and our reason for being, and so must be injurious to us.

Three and a half years equates to separation from God, but Jesus' three and a half years of ministry which culminated in His death for our sins, cancels the separation and brings hope to a lost world, The time is made up, the debt is paid, reconciliation is achieved, and through salvation, we experience harmony with God once again.

Revelation Chapter Twelve

THE WOMAN AND THE GREAT RED DRAGON

Based on Revelation 12:1-17

From Revelation chapter one we have been examining God's church through the ages; its development, and changing characteristics; the earthly powers attacking it; God's judgements on the powers persecuting it. Now, in Revelation 12 our attention focuses on the supernatural puppeteer orchestrating the attacks on God's people.

Revelation 12:1-2 – John sees a great wonder or sign in heaven. It is a woman clothed with the sun, standing on the moon, and wearing a crown of twelve stars. She is heavily pregnant and about to give birth.

This wonder is rich in symbolism and needs deciphering. Let us look at the description in detail and use the Bible to interpret each facet:

- **A great sign appeared in heaven**
  Genesis 1:1 tells us that God created the *"heavens"*. Therefore, there is more than one heaven. Genesis 1:6-8 tell of the creation of the atmosphere (or sky), and Genesis 1:14-17 describe the starry heavens. Then, in 2 Corinthians 12:2-4, Paul tells of a man who was taken into vision and caught up to the *"third heaven"*, which he describes as *"paradise"*, where he was given a message by God. When we put these Bible texts together, we can conclude there are actually three heavens; the atmosphere (sky), the starry heavens, and the heaven where God dwells. As the woman in Revelation 12:1 is clothed with the sun, moon and stars, it seems the great sign appears in the starry heavens.

- **A woman**

  The following Bible texts describe God's people, or His church, as a virtuous woman (Jeremiah 6:2, Isaiah 54:5,6, 2 Corinthians 11:2, Ephesians 5:23-27, Ephesians 5:31,32).

- **Clothed with the sun**

  The following texts compare the sun; the physical light of the world, to Jesus, the *"Sun of Righteousness"*; the spiritual light of the world (Malachi 4:2, Luke 1:78,79, John 8:12, John 9:5).

- **The moon under her feet**

  Just as the moon reflects the light of the sun, so the Word of God (The Bible) reflects the Light of the World, Jesus, (see John 5:39, 46-47, Luke 24:27,44). The woman rests her feet on the moon (for it is her foundation), thus the Bible, which teaches about Christ, is the foundation of the church's beliefs (see John 5:39).

- **Crown of twelve stars**

  A crown signifies rulership. We come across the number twelve many times in Revelation; it always denotes spiritual perfection or completion. Twelve has special significance for God's people in Bible times. In the Old Testament, ancient Israel had twelve tribes, and the nation was led by twelve judges. In the New Testament, we have the twelve apostles who led the early Christian church. Revelation 1:20 identifies the stars, being held by Jesus, as the leaders of His churches. As the woman wears a crown of twelve stars this reminds us that the church of God has been consistently led by a spiritually complete group of twelve.

- **The woman is pregnant and about to give birth**

  Isaiah 26:17 describes God's people about to give birth.

The wonder seen by John is a description of God's church. Throughout time, there has always been a group of people who worship the true God. Once again, Jesus has a story to tell of His people.

135

Revelation 12:3-4 – In this story, another character is revealed to John. It is an enormous red dragon. And again, the Bible will interpret who this dragon symbolises, as follows:

- **Enormous red dragon**
  We do not have to go far for the identification of the enormous red dragon, Revelation 12:9 tells us it is the devil; also known as *"that ancient serpent"* and *"Satan"*. The name 'ancient serpent' has great significance for it identifies the devil as the serpent in the Garden of Eden who caused sin to come into the world (see Genesis 3). If you want to know who to blame for the sorry condition of our planet, you need go no further. The devil is responsible for it all.

- **The dragon has seven heads and ten horns**
  Revelation 17:10,12 tell us that, when dealing with Bible prophecy, heads and horns of beasts signify rulers or kings.

- **Seven crowns on its heads**
  A further reference to royal rulers.
  The prophecies of Daniel chapters 7 and 8, and Revelation chapters 13 and 17, show beasts with heads, horns and crowns that symbolise rulers or kingdoms. The enormous red dragon (the devil) is also shown as having multiple heads, horns and crowns, and as we will see in Revelation 13, this signifies that in his terrible work on planet earth, he does not reveal himself as the devil, but hides behind earthly kings and rulers. He is a master of deception and, as the greatest deceiver that has ever lived, he utilises others to do his dirty work on his behalf. As stated by John Wilkinson in his book 'Quakerism Examined', *"One of the artifices of Satan is, to induce men to believe that he does not exist . . ."*

Revelation 12 cuts through the smokescreen of deception and reveals there certainly is a devil, and he is working efficiently, albeit behind the scenes, through his chosen agencies - earth's mighty rulers.

- **Its tail swept a third of the stars out of the sky and flung them to the earth** Revelation 12:9 explains who these stars are: they are the angels thrown out of heaven with the devil before the earth was created (more on this later). Isaiah 9:15 tells us a tail represents the lies of a false prophet. Therefore, the devil was able to deceive one-third of the angels in heaven and cause their decline (see also Jude 6, 2 Peter 2:4).

Now we are clear, the enormous red dragon is the devil. But what is his relationship to the woman (the church of God)?

138

Revelation 12:4 - The dragon stood in front of the woman who was about to give birth, so that it might devour her child the moment he was born. We already know the woman is about to deliver a child. We now know it is a male child, and the devil is awaiting the baby's delivery, so he can destroy Him before He has a chance to grow up. The woman and the devil, also called *"that ancient serpent"* (see Revelation 12:9) have history together. They are sworn enemies, and have been since the beginning.

Genesis 3 depicts the fall of Adam and Eve, brought about by the devil (using the serpent as his medium). He deceived Eve into eating the forbidden fruit from the Tree of the Knowledge of Good and Evil. Mercifully, God promised Eve that a man from her seed would crush the head of the serpent, in other words, cause the serpent's death (see Genesis 3:15), although the serpent would be able to bruise the man's heal.

Jesus, the Son of Man (and Son of God) did indeed come through Eve's seed. Born as a man, He came through the seed, not only of Eve, but also of her descendant, Abraham (see Luke 3:23-38). In Genesis 12:2,3 (see also Galatians 3:16) we see Abraham also receiving God's promise of the Messiah coming through his lineage. This further promise to Abraham, the *"father of all who believe"* (Romans 4:11), aptly shows how Jesus, the male child of Revelation 12, was symbolically born from God's church.

Revelation 12:4 prophesies that the dragon will attempt to devour the woman's child as soon as it is born. Did the devil try to kill the infant Jesus? Yes, Matthew 2 tells the well-known story of the Magi, who reported to king Herod their search for the baby boy, born to become the king of the Jews. Herod then, in an effort to kill Jesus, ordered the mass murder of all infant boys in Bethlehem.

Revelation 12:5 - foretells that the devil, the instigator of Herod's horrific murder spree, would fail in his attempt to kill the special child. The murder of the innocents reveals the true nature of the devil. He uses those in power to slaughter the guiltless, in order to achieve his objectives. This is a work he is still engaged in today. Jesus lived to carry out His mission of providing salvation for humanity. He was crucified, and died for our sins (fulfilling the promise of His being bruised), but He rose from the dead in triumph, having gained victory over sin and death. And, not only that, this man-child was destined to *"rule all the nations with an iron sceptre"* (see also Psalm 2:7-9). Therefore, after His resurrection, Jesus was caught up to heaven to His throne where He now sits at the right hand of His Father (see Hebrews 1:3). The completion of the plan of salvation effectively sentenced the devil to death, as promised in Genesis 3. (We will see this sentence carried out in Revelation 20.)

Revelation 12:6 – Now that Jesus is out of reach, the devil turns his murderous attention to the woman (the church of God). She has to flee into the wilderness to a place prepared for her by God, where she can be nurtured for 1,260 days. Here is more symbolic language to be interpreted:

- **The church flees into the wilderness**
  The church is being persecuted by the devil and has to go into hiding in a barren place, away from public view. It is in exile, and must go underground in order to survive: God has prepared a place for its preservation.

- **1,260 days**
  Again, we are given prophetic time. We know that in Bible prophecy time periods are governed by the day/year principle: one prophetic day equals one literal year (see Ezekiel 4:6). Therefore, 1,260 prophetic days equal 1,260 literal years. We came across this 1,260 year period in Revelation chapter eleven. This time of persecution for God's church also appears in various forms in other parts of the Bible:
  - 1,260 days (Revelation 11:3, 12:6)
  - 42 months (Revelation 11:2, 13:5)
  - 3.1/2 times (Daniel 7:25, 12:7, Revelation 12:14).

The historical period of 1,260 years, when the church of God was persecuted by the Papacy (the Church of Rome), identified as an agent of the devil in Revelation 13, is commonly known as the Dark Ages (AD538 – 1798). This period saw millions of people martyred for their Christian faith. It included the Crusades, the Spanish Inquisition, the reign of Mary Tudor (Bloody Mary), Protestant martyrs killed during the Reformation, and many more atrocities. It is estimated that in the Inquisition alone, 50-68 million people were killed by the Roman Catholic Church, during the 1,260 years. (www.themichigancatholic.org) However, as promised, God's church was not wiped out. He preserved His church in the barren places of Europe.

The Waldenses, originating in the 12th Century in France, and the Albigenses originating in the 12th and 13th Centuries in Southern France, were Protestant groups who vigorously opposed the Catholic Church, and were persecuted as a result. They fled to the wilderness to escape Catholic tyranny. By the 15th Century the Waldenses were confined mostly to the French and Italian valleys of the Cottian Alps. (www.britannica/com/topic/Waldenses)

Large numbers of Albigenses could be found in the ancient mountainous regions of Vivarais, Anvergne and the Jura mountains in Burgundy. ('Were the Albigenses and Waldenses forerunners of the Reformation?' Daniel Walther)

Revelation 12:7-9 – The scene now changes. We are given a flashback which answers the question - Why does the enormous red dragon (the devil) hate the woman (God's church), and her child (Jesus)?

The answer is given in the form of a true story that took place before the earth was created; before Jesus became a human baby; and before the devil became the devil.

Isaiah 14:12 and Ezekiel 28:12-19 tell us that the devil was once a beautiful angel called Lucifer (the bearer of light). He was a covering Cherub, who stood in the very presence of God. It is a great mystery that, in heaven, a place where there is no sin, wickedness emerged and developed within this exalted being, and corrupted him. Instead of resisting the poisonous canker, Lucifer cherished it, until it consumed him. As shown in Revelation 12:4, Lucifer sought allies. He deceived one-third of the angelic host, persuaded them to join his rebellion, and began a war in heaven.

Revelation 12:7 - tells us that a war broke out in heaven between Michael and His angels, and the dragon (the devil) and his angels.

Who is Michael? The name means 'Who is like God', and Daniel 10:21 and 12:1 identify Michael respectively as *"Your Prince"* and *"The Great Prince"*. Jude 9 identifies Michael as the Archangel, and 1 Thessalonians 4:16 and John 5:25 tell us that at the Second Coming Jesus will use His Archangel voice to resurrect the dead to life. These texts indicate Michael is the name used by Jesus, especially when He is in fighting mode. Of course, Jesus is not an angel (see Hebrews 1); He is The Archangel, the Commander of the heavenly host. Therefore, we see Him in Revelation 12:7 leading His loyal angels in battle against the devil and his deceived angels.

Revelation 12:8-9 - tell us the dragon was weaker than Jesus, and therefore lost the battle. Consequently, Lucifer could no longer retain his name, he became Satan, the enemy of God, and both he and his angels forfeited their place in heaven. They were hurled down, and made their home on earth. From his base here, the devil leads the whole world astray. Thus, we have the tragic story of the fall of our first parents, Adam and Eve. The devil, with his angels, was able to set up camp on earth, because Adam and Eve believed his lies, and disobeyed God. Since that time, the devil has sought to deceive every human being. No doubt, if Adam and Eve had resisted Satan's temptation, trusted God, and remained loyal to Him, the devil would have been banished from the earth, and the awful results of sin would not be the legacy we all have to live with today.

Revelation 12:10 - is a declaration. John hears a loud voice from heaven proclaiming Jesus has won. He won not only the battle in heaven, but also the battle against sin, brought to this earth by the devil. By His sinless life, His death in our place, which satisfied the penalty for sin, and His resurrection, that guarantees eternal life for all who accept His salvation, Jesus has once again conquered the devil and His angels. No longer is the devil able to accuse God's people of being unworthy to attain eternal life. For, their acceptance of Jesus, and His sacrifice for their sins, gives them a free pass into heaven, from where the devil was hurled down, and to where he can never return. No wonder the devil is mad with the woman (God's church), and with her child (Jesus), who is able to defeat him, whether in heavenly fighting mode as Michael the great Archangel, or a defenceless human being living on earth. It is as if the devil has been hurled down twice; once physically out of heaven, and then eternally from the hearts of human beings.

Revelation 12:11 – tells us humanity triumphs over the devil by being covered by the blood of the Lamb – that is, they accept the sacrifice of Jesus. They also triumph by the word of their testimony, which is their proclamation of the change Jesus has wrought in their lives. By this testimony, they bear witness of their victory over sin's control. For, to follow Jesus is to be changed into His image, and live as He lived. These human beings are willing to give up their lives for their faith, so strong is their relationship with Jesus. There is nothing the devil can do to break their attachment to Jesus, and the salvation He provides.

Revelation 12:12 – But, then we receive a warning. All those in heaven can rejoice because they are free of the devil and his deceptive work. However, we on earth must beware; for the devil, although thoroughly defeated, will not give up his evil stratagem. On the contrary, he is furious. He knows his card is marked, his time is limited, and his eternal destruction has been appointed. Therefore, he is determined to take as many human beings with him into hell fire as he possibly can.

The devil is familiar with the nature of God. He knows God will not force anyone to act against their will. Satan understands that in order for humans to be saved they must choose salvation. Therefore, his work is to deceive them into disregarding the saving of their souls. He paints the road to hell as the more desirable choice; a way of freedom and self-determination. Of course, this is a lie, but so many of us will be deceived. The truth is, happiness now, and throughout eternity, can only be achieved in a loving and obedient relationship with Jesus. The so-called freedom offered by the devil is a myth that leads to self-destruction.

Since the devil is well aware that his time is short, he has redoubled his efforts to destroy humanity. He has determined he will not go into the fire alone.

Revelation 12:13-14 - bring us back to the original story of the enormous red dragon pursuing the woman. The dragon has been hurled to the earth, and now the man-child (Jesus), is back in heaven out of reach. Therefore, his only recourse is to pursue the woman. Moreover, as we have already learned, the devil oppresses the church for a specific period (1,260 years), while God protects the existence of His church in desolate places. The church is given wings to escape. Exodus 19:4 and Deuteronomy 32:11 show God carrying His people on speedy eagles' wings in order to transport them to safety. This time, the 1,260 year period is shown as *"Time, times and half a time"* (three and a half times), however this is the same time period.

Three and a half times (in other words three and a half years) is once again prophetic time, and we can calculate it as follows:

- The ancient Jewish calendar (or BLC) has 30 days in each of its 12 months. Therefore, one year is 360 days (12 x 30);
- As one year has 360 days, then 3 years is 3 x 360 = **1,080** days;
- half a year is **180** days (360 divided by 2);
- 1,080 plus 180 = 1,260 days;
- Therefore, in 3.1/2 years there are 1,260 days.

As we know, for prophetic time, one prophetic day = one literal year (see Ezekiel 4:6).

Therefore, 1,260 prophetic days = 1,260 literal years.

Once again, we have the 1,260 years of Papal persecution, as shown in Revelation 12:6 - The Dark Ages, AD538 – 1798.

The following quotations are from 'Ecclesiastical Empire', Alonzo T Jones, chapter XII,

"In the year 532, Justinian issued an edict declaring his intention 'to unite all men in one faith'. Whether they were Jews, Gentiles, or Christians, all who did not within three months profess and embrace the Catholic faith, were by the edict 'declared infamous, and as such excluded from all employments both civil and military; rendered incapable of leaving anything by will; and all their estates confiscated, whether real or personal.' As a result of this cruel edict, great numbers were driven from their habitations with their wives and children, stripped and naked. Others betook themselves to flight, carrying with them what they could conceal, for their support and maintenance, but they were plundered of what little they had, and many of them inhumanly massacred.

"By 538 AD the Church of Rome had full supremacy. The longer time went on the less safe it was to live or mingle in populated areas where one could easily be recognised as or found out to be a so called heretic. To teach contrary to or stand up against the Papal Power could very easily and most likely result in the

death of the so called offender. The only safety was in the mountainous regions and places of obscurity to where God's Church fled."

Revelation 12:15 – The devil, now described as one of his other personas *"the serpent"*, uses water to destroy the church. He actually spews water from his mouth like a river in order to sweep God's church away with a torrent. In Bible prophecy, water is symbolic of multitudes of people, from different nations (see Revelation 17:15). Therefore, the serpent uses various nations, to destroy God's people. This is borne out by history, as, during the 1,260 year period the Crusades took place. Here is a list of some of the Crusades in Europe during 1095 to 1492:

- Crusade against the Celtic Christians in Britain;
- Crusade against the non-Catholic Christians of Thrace;
- Crusade against the Ostrogoths in Italy;
- Crusades against the Waldenses in Northern Italy;
- Crusade against the Albigenses in southern and western France;
- Crusade in Ireland by Henry II of England with the support of the Papacy;
- Crusade against the Lollards in England (the followers of John Wycliffe);
- Crusade against Spanish Protestants at the time of the Spanish Inquisition;
- Crusade against the Hussites (the followers of John Huss in Bohemia);
- Crusade against German Protestants at the time of the Reformation;
- Crusade against Swiss Protestants by Catholic Authorities;
- Crusade against Dutch Protestants by Philip II of Spain;
- Crusade against English Protestants by the Spanish Armada;
- Crusade against French Protestants called Huguenots in the St Bartholomew massacre;

All of the above were either led or supported by the Church of Rome. (www.revelationbibleprophecy.org/revelation12)

Revelation 12:16 – The earth helped the woman by opening its mouth and swallowing the river that the dragon spewed out of his mouth.

History helps us here in identifying how God's people escaped the deluge of persecution facing them during this time.

First, let us look at the symbol of the earth. If we accept that earth is the opposite of sea, and, as we already know from Revelation 17:15 that seas (or a great torrent of water), in prophecy, mean a multitude of people, then it follows that the earth represents a sparsely populated area. Therefore, as the 1,260 year period was coming to an end, when the church was terribly oppressed, and only survived by hiding in the mountainous regions in Europe, there would come a time when many of the persecuted Protestants would flee to a sparsely populated country to find safety and religious freedom. And, so it happened, that on 6 September 1620 the Pilgrim Fathers sailed from Plymouth (England) to Massachusetts in North America. They were the Founding Fathers who would lead the way for many others fleeing Papal persecution in Europe. In this way, the earth (sparsely populated North America) swallowed up the river torrent (many persecuting European nations), and God's church found refuge.

Revelation 12:17 - Again, the devil's plan was thwarted. In his fury, he had sought to destroy God's church. Defeated by Jesus in heaven; defeated by Jesus on earth; and unable to defeat God's church in Europe, instead of giving up, he became enraged. He decided to wage war against the church's children, her remnant (those that remain). In other words, this prophecy now becomes relevant for those living towards the end of time, identified as the remnant children of God. They look exactly like the woman we met in Revelation 12:1. They are also clothed with the righteousness of Jesus, and use the Bible as their foundation. They wear the crown of twelve stars; showing their connection with the spiritually complete church of old.

Revelation 12:17 further describes the remnant as keeping the commandments of God and holding fast to their testimony about Jesus.

Here are the identifying characteristics of God's true church on earth now, with whom the devil is particularly angry. God's church will keep all His commandments, and also bear witness to Jesus as God and Saviour. Revelation 19:10 further defines the *"testimony to Jesus"* as the *"Spirit of prophecy"*. Therefore, God's church can also be identified as having the gift of prophecy in its midst. Just as in Old Testament times when God's prophets guided His church, so His church at the end of time will be guided by His prophets.

The devil has not changed. He is waging outright war against these people, but the good news is, Satan has failed to win any war he has staged. He is truly a defeated foe. Therefore, the weakest sinner, who holds on to Jesus as his/her Saviour, will find themselves on the winning side.

Revelation Chapter Thirteen

THE UNHOLY TRINITY

Based on Revelation 13:1-18

In Revelation chapter thirteen we are introduced to the Unholy Trinity; a counterfeit of the Holy Trinity – Father, Son and Holy Spirit. The false father figure of the counterfeit trinity, we have already met in Revelation chapter twelve. He is the great red dragon, the devil. We have yet to meet the false Son (although we know his work), and the false Holy Spirit, who is alive and kicking in the last days of earth's history. Revelation 13 unveils these counterfeits so that none of us need be deceived.

In Revelation 12 we saw God's church, depicted as a virtuous woman, fleeing from the great red dragon, identified as the devil. The devil has lost the war against Jesus in heaven, and has failed to destroy God's church on earth. By chapter 13 the great red dragon is furious. He needs to come up with a new plan that will succeed. In Revelation 13:1 we find him standing on the shore of the sea awaiting the rise of his new medium, to whom he will give his power, and authority, and through whom he will wreak havoc on God's church, and the whole world.

Revelation 13:1-2 - show a new beast with very specific characteristics, all of which are clues to who this beast represents. We will use the Bible to interpret each characteristic:

- **It is a beast**
  Daniel 7:17 tells us that in prophecy great beasts represent great kings or kingdoms.

- **It comes out of the sea**
  Revelation 17:15 tells us that sea represents densely populated areas.

- **It has 10 horns**
  Daniel 7:24 tells us that horns represent kings.

- **The beast has seven heads**
  In Daniel 2:36-38, as Daniel is interpreting King Nebuchadnezzar's dream, he identifies the head of a great statue as King Nebuchadnezzar himself and Babylon, the nation he rules. Daniel says to Nebuchadnezzar *"You are that head of gold."* Also, in Daniel's own dream in Daniel chapter seven, he sees four beasts. The third beast is a leopard (the world dominating kingdom of Greece), with four heads, which represent the four generals who continued Grecian rule after the death of Alexander the Great (Daniel 7:6). We can therefore conclude that when interpreting prophecy, heads are symbols of kings or rulers, and the kingdoms they represent.

- **Each head has a blasphemous name**
  One school of thought is that the seven heads of this beast represent the seven major powers opposing God's people through the ages, namely, Egypt, Assyria, Babylon, Medo-Persia, Greece, Pagan Rome, Papal Rome. Each of these nations ruled in opposition to God and therefore could comfortably wear a blasphemous name.

- **The beast has ten crowns on its horns**
  Surely this confirms that the horns are indeed kings for they are wearing crowns. More specifically, we could conclude that these are the ten kings who ruled the nations of Europe after the fall of Imperial Rome, as shown in Daniel 7:24.

- **The beast resembled a leopard, but had feet like a bear and a lion's mouth**
  In Daniel 7:4-6 Daniel's dream shows the kingdoms of Babylon, Medo-Persia and Greece represented respectively as a lion, bear and leopard. Again, these are world ruling empires that opposed God.

We can now identify the beast of Revelation 13 as the embodiment of the great nations of Egypt, Assyria, Babylon, Medo-Persia, Greece, Pagan Rome, Papal Rome, who through the ages have ruled in opposition to God. As we will see, the last of these nations, Papal Rome, is the power that most fulfils the actions of this beast. It follows the line of world ruling empires that have oppressed God's people, but it surpasses each of its predecessors in its zeal to continue the devil's persecution of God's church. Because of its appearance, Bible scholars refer to this beast as the leopard-like beast.

Revelation 13:2 - The dragon gives his power, throne and authority to the leopard-like beast. The power, and puppeteer, behind this blasphemous ruler is the devil himself. This is confirmed by how closely the beast resembles the great red dragon. In Revelation 12:3 the great red dragon is identified as having seven heads and ten horns, just as the leopard-like beast of Revelation 13.

It is interesting that the great red dragon has crowns on its seven heads, whilst the leopard-like beast has crowns on its ten horns (Revelation 13:1). As both the seven heads and ten horns represent kingdoms ruled by kings who oppose God, the images still agree. However, the different positions of crowns can be explained, as we will see later.

The similarity of seven heads and ten horns is striking. In John 14:9 when Jesus was explaining to his disciples the similarity between Himself and God the Father, He said *"Anyone who has seen Me has seen the Father."* And so it is with the devil (the counterfeit Father), and the leopard-like beast (the counterfeit Son). The leopard-like beast looks like its father, the devil. It receives its power, throne and authority from him, and carries out his work.

Revelation 13:3 – One of the beast's seven heads has a fatal wound. In other words, a wound that should lead to death. However, the fatal wound is healed, and because of this, the whole world is filled with wonder, and follows the beast.

Here is another counterfeit characteristic. As the false Christ, this leopard-like beast receives a deadly wound but raises from the dead. This is truly a poor imitation of Jesus, the true Christ, who died for our sins, and was resurrected on the third day.

Revelation 13:4 – It is clear that although people are directing their adoration and worship to the leopard-like beast, in actual fact they are worshiping the great red dragon (the devil); for he is the one pulling the strings of the beast. The mention of worship here indicates the beast is not only a political ruler, but also a religious power, for it accepts worship. This is further evidence that the final form of the beast represents Papal Rome, which superseded Pagan Rome. Papal Rome was an amalgamation of political government and religion. It came to power amidst the densely populated nations of Europe, and so is pictured as rising from the sea (a prophetic symbol for multitudes of people). Indeed, Papal Rome fits each characteristic so far.

Revelation 13:5-7 – The actions of the leopard-like beast are highlighted. They bear close resemblance to those of the Little Horn power of Daniel 7, as shown in the following table:

Actions of the leopard-like beast of Revelation 13:	Actions of the Little Horn of Daniel 7:
• It is given a mouth to utter proud words; • It blasphemes (speaks against God); • It slanders God's name; • It slanders God's dwelling place; • It slanders those who live in heaven;	• The horn has a human mouth that speaks boastfully; • It will speak against the Most High; • It will try to change the set times and laws;

Actions of the leopard-like beast of Revelation 13:	Actions of the Little Horn of Daniel 7:
• It is given power to wage war against God's holy people and conquer them;	• It will oppress God's holy people; • It wages war against the holy people and defeats them;
• It exercises its authority for 42 months;	• The holy people will be delivered into his hands for a time, times and half a time.
• It is given authority over the whole world.	

As we can see, both powers behave identically, but are they the same power? We are helped in coming to a conclusion because both the leopard-like beast and the Little Horn reign supremely for a specific period of time. And, as in Revelation chapter twelve, we are dealing with prophetic time in both instances. Therefore, the day/year principle of one prophetic day equals one literal year (see Ezekiel 4:6) must once again apply.

The beast of Revelation 13 rules for **42 months**. The Little Horn of Daniel 7 rules for **time, times and half a time (3.1/2 times).**

We have come across this 3.1/2 times before in Revelation 12:14 (see previous chapter) where we calculated this prophetic time period as **1,260 literal years.**

Now we can calculate the 42 months of Revelation 13:5, as follows:

In the ancient Jewish calendar (or BLC) each of its 12 months has 30 days. Therefore, 42 months has 1,260 days (42 x 30). As we are dealing with prophetic time (one prophetic day equals one literal year [see Ezekiel 4:6]), then **1,260 prophetic days equal 1,260 literal years.**

Just as identified in Revelation 12, we are dealing with the infamous 1,260 years of Papal supremacy (AD538 – 1798), the Dark Ages when, anyone refusing to acknowledge as supreme, and worship the Roman Catholic Church was hunted, persecuted, tortured, and ultimately killed. It is therefore safe to conclude that the leopard-like beast of Revelation 13 and the Little Horn of Daniel 7 are one and the same, the Papal Power - the Roman Catholic Church.

Let us now return to the difference between the physical appearance of the great red dragon (the devil), and the leopard-like beast of Revelation 13.

As we have discovered, heads and horns in Bible prophecy are interchangeable; they both signify kings, rulers and nations. Both the dragon and the leopard-like beast have seven heads and ten horns. The seven heads can be identified as the seven prominent nations through time that have opposed God. The dragon has crowns on its seven heads, so this explanation fits. However, the leopard-like beast has crowns on its ten horns, not its heads. This indicates the leopard-like beast's emergence as Papal Rome takes place during the rule of the ten kings. And this is exactly what took place. Daniel 7:8,20,24 tell of the rise of the Papacy, that emerged during the reign of the ten European nations, which ruled following the fall of Imperial Rome. Therefore, when Papal Rome came to power, the ten European rulers, symbolised by the beast's ten horns, were wearing their crowns. The Roman Church's rise to supremacy took place in AD527 when the Bishop of Rome was legally made the head of all holy churches.

As we learned in Revelation 13:3, the Papacy would suffer a deadly wound. This happened at the end of the Dark Ages in 1798 when Napoleon's General Berthier took the Pope (Pius VI) into captivity. In 1870 the Papal States were absorbed into Italy, and it was decreed that no successor would be allowed to take the Pope's place. Effectively, it was the death of the Papacy. However, that is not the end of the story, for although the Papacy 'died' in 1798, the Catholic Church continued to elect Popes who remained out of public sight in voluntary exile, as prisoners of the State.

Revelation 13:3 also prophesies that the beast's fatal injury would be healed. This part of the prophecy is still in progress. It began in 1929 when Mussolini, in the Lateran Treaty, restored power to the Pope (Pius X1), who was given rule of the Vatican City. The Lateran Treaty is still in force today. Therefore, the deadly wound is definitely healing.

The prophecy states the wound will be completely healed, and the whole world will once again wonder after the beast. The Dark Ages were the dreadful result of the world following the leopard-like beast, and the same results will ensue when the deadly wound is fully healed.

Here are some evidences of the healing of the deadly wound in our time:

In 1984 the United States established diplomatic relations with the Vatican.

In 1987 the president of the United States (Ronald Reagan) welcomed Pope John Paul II to preach to the American people: He said *"As you exhort us, we will listen. For with all our hearts we yearn to make this good land better still."* The next day 27 Protestant and Eastern Orthodox leaders met with the Pope in Columbia, South Carolina. A few days later in Los Angeles, he met with representatives of Islam, Hinduism, Buddhism and Judaism. In the previous year (1986) hundreds of leaders of all the major world religions joined with the Pope in Italy, at his request, in a specific prayer service for world peace. ('Signs of the Times' - December 1987 page 21)

Moreover, every successive US President has met with the officiating Pope to make alliances, including Donald Trump who first met with Pope Francis on 24 May 2017, when they consulted on terrorism and climate change. The Pope is treated not only as the world's greatest religious leader but also as a global political spokesman, whose views are sought on every issue. Francis has become the most popular moral voice in the world. Christians of every denomination, and non-Christians alike, admire and give attention to his declarations.

In October 2017, one week before the 500 year anniversary of the start of the Reformation, when prominent Catholics like Martin Luther broke away from the Catholic Church in order to form the Protestant movement, Pope Francis, in an interview, stated that Catholics and Protestants were now enjoying a relationship of *"true fraternity"* based on mutual understanding, trust and co-operation. He went on to say that the two traditions were *"no longer...adversaries, after long centuries of estrangement and conflict."* ('The Guardian website' – 'Catholic and Protestant leaders unite to mark start of Reformation')

As we have already seen in Revelation 13:4, the prophecy warns that those who worship the leopard-like beast are, in reality, worshiping the devil: for it is the devil who has given the beast his power, throne and authority. Moreover, the beast's rise on the world stage will once again result in oppression and persecution. History will repeat itself.

Revelation 13:8 - tells us that although all inhabitants of the earth will worship the leopard-like beast, there will be a group who refuse to do so. They are the ones whose names are written in the Lamb's book of life. And, we have come across this Lamb before in Revelation chapter five. He is none other than Jesus, the Saviour of the world. All those who follow Jesus (the true Messiah) will refuse to follow the leopard-like beast (the counterfeit Messiah) and will suffer dire consequences for their decision.

Revelation 13:9-10 – God gives a warning to His saints living through the Dark Ages. There will be casualties, for great numbers of His people will be martyred for their faith. It may appear the wicked (those who follow the leopard-like beast) are winning, but Just as with the souls under the altar in Revelation chapter six, who cry out *"How long... Lord?"* God answers, *"...wait a little longer"*. Justice is coming. He confirms that His people, living at this time of persecution, will need patient endurance and faithfulness to face this unprecedented ordeal.

Now that we have identified the leopard-like beast that rises from the sea, Revelation 13 introduces another beast, this time rising from the land. Here is the counterfeit Holy Spirit.

Revelation 13:11 - John sees a second beast. As we have already proved, beasts in prophecy signify kingdoms. This kingdom, however, emerges from the earth. If seas are symbolic of densely populated regions, then we can conclude earth symbolises sparsely populated areas.

This beast has two horns (like a lamb) but it speaks like a dragon. Horns on prophetic beasts usually symbolise kings or rulers, however in this case, there is a significant difference, for the horns are part of the description of the beast itself. It has the horns of a lamb, yet it speaks like a dragon. In other words, at first glance, this beast appears to be as gentle and harmless as a lamb, but in reality, it is a dragon we must fear. Or perhaps, when it arose as a New World power it had all the appearance of the Lamb of God (Jesus), but as time passes, it takes on the persona of the great red dragon (the devil) and begins to speak like him.

There is a nation, formally founded on 4 July 1776, that established its constitution in 1791, around the time the leopard-like beast (the Papacy) was receiving its deadly wound. This nation was sparsely populated at the time. It came into being as a haven for Protestants fleeing Catholic persecution in Europe. It began as a great champion of religious and civil liberties, but it has grown into the most influential nation on earth, with its fingers in the affairs of every country of the world, and powerful beyond measure. This nation is the United States of America (USA).

Revelation 13:12 – This lamb-like beast exercises all the authority of the leopard-like beast before it. Thus, the second beast (the USA), acts on behalf of the first beast (the Papacy). And, as the Papacy received its authority from the devil, then it follows that the USA is also being controlled by Satan. The lamb-like beast compels the world to worship the leopard-like beast. We are now viewing our future. The prophecy states, the USA will cause the whole world to worship the Papacy.

The USA is a Protestant country. The Pilgrim Fathers fled Catholic persecution and found refuge in the United States. Its constitution strongly promotes freedom of worship, and the separation of church and State, ensuring its citizens cannot be persecuted for their faith. And yet, this very nation, built upon such honourable principles, will aid, abet, and act in the same way as the greatest persecutor of all time.

Revelation 13:13-15 - Here are the details of how the second beast (the lamb-like beast) will become the ambassador of the first beast (the leopard-like beast). First, the lamb-like beast will perform miracles *"causing fire to come down from heaven"* which everyone will see, and be deceived by. People will be drawn to the power of this beast because of what it can do.

The actions of the lamb-like beast imitate those of the Holy Spirit. In Acts 2:1-4 we see the Holy Spirit descending on the early apostles in the form of tongues of fire. The lamb-like beast will also cause fire to come down from heaven. This time, the purpose is not to equip God's people to spread the gospel, but to deceive the whole world into worshiping the Papacy.

Second, the lamb-like beast will set up an image to the first beast and cause the image to come to life. All who refuse to worship the living image will be killed. What is this image that comes to life?

As with any image, it must look like the original. And, as this is a living image, it will behave just like the original. In Revelation 13:5-7 we saw how the leopard-like beast behaved; it blasphemed God; slandered His name, heaven and all who live there; waged war against God's people and conquered them. Also, Daniel 7:25 adds, the Papacy sought to change times and laws. The Roman Catholic Church has indeed tried to change the law of God. In the Ten Commandments given to the Children of Israel in the wilderness (see Exodus 20:2-12), the second commandment forbids the worship of idols. Yet the Catholic Church promotes idol worship. Statues of Jesus, Mary, the Apostles, and the appointed saints, decorate Catholic churches, and are on sale to all who wish to purchase them. The act of praying to these idols is encouraged by the Church. Yet the Bible states our prayers must only be directed to God, our Father (see Matthew 6:9).

Also, the fourth commandment instructs us to keep holy the seventh-day Sabbath as a memorial of God's creation of the heavens and earth. Yet the Catholic Church instructs its followers to keep the first day of the week (Sunday) holy as a memorial of Jesus' resurrection, and proudly admits it has no scriptural permission to make this change. The Church boasts that it needs no Biblical authorisation to do this, as its own authority allows it to alter God's word. Surely, this is the blasphemy against God stated in Revelation 13:6. The Catholic Church is not shy in proclaiming its right to amend the law of God, and, the time He has instituted for worship.

Please see the following two quotations:
'The Augsburg Confession' Lutheran statement presented to the emperor at the Diet of Augsberg, 1530:

"They (the Catholics) allege the Sabbath changed into Sunday, the Lord's day, contrary to the Decalogue, as it appears; neither is there any example more boasted of than the changing of the Sabbath day, Great, say they, is the power and authority of the church, since it dispensed with one of the ten commandments." (Article xxviii)

In a letter written in November 1895, Mr H F Thomas, chancellor to Cardinal Gibbons, replying to an inquiry as to whether the Catholic Church claims to have changed the Sabbath, said *"Of course the Catholic church claims that the change was her act . . . and the act is a mark of her ecclesiastical authority in religious things."* (Quotations taken from Sabbath School Lessons 'Present Triumph, Future Glory' July-Sept 1989)

The defining mark of the Catholic Church is its claim to possess the power to change the law that God instituted, without God's permission to do so. It has decreed that the Sabbath is now Sunday, and the majority of Protestant churches follow its lead in worshiping on the first day of the week.

We can therefore conclude that the image to the Roman Catholic Church, set up by the USA, will be a church that, whilst being Protestant, will look and act like the Catholic Church. Revelation 13:15 further states that empowered by the Papacy, the US Protestant Church will seek to put to death all people who refuse to adhere to its dictates, which of course are, in reality, the dictates of the Catholic Church. These dictates will include the Catholic Church's flag ship – Sunday worship.

Revelation 13:16-17 – The USA Protestant Church will have the full backing of the USA government; for it has the power to force *"all people, great and small, rich and poor, free and slave, to receive a mark on their right hands or on their foreheads, so that they cannot buy or sell unless they have the mark . . ."*.

It is clear that laws will be instituted in order to make people worship the USA Protestant church, which is no more than an image of the Roman Catholic Church. Those who obey these laws will be given a mark. This mark is identified as *"the name of the beast or the number of its name."*

There is much speculation regarding the 'mark of the beast'. A quick Internet search brings up all kinds of theories. Many believe the mark is a literal stamp or barcode placed on the right hand or forehead, or even a microchip injected under the skin. Following the COVID-19 pandemic, the latest theory appears to be the transmission of a microchip through a vaccine. However, as we are told 'all people' on earth receive this mark, which of course would have to be indelible, it seems unlikely this could be implemented for a global population of almost 8 billion people.

Let us stick with what the Bible says, and bear in mind, Revelation is a symbolic book. The fact that some receive the mark on their right hands, and some on their foreheads, will certainly be significant. Furthermore, Revelation 13:17 says the mark is *"the name of the beast or the number of its name"*. This must also be significant. As we have proved, in its latter stage, the leopard-like beast symbolises the Roman Catholic Church. It follows, then, that the mark of the beast will represent the Catholic Church.

As already stated, the defining act of the Papacy is its change of the day of worship from Saturday to Sunday, which most Protestant churches accept and practice. If the latter day US Protestant Church, supported by the US government, were to institute a law forcing everyone to worship on Sunday, this certainly would be a fitting way of acknowledging the supremacy of the leopard-like beast from the sea. Moreover, as Revelation 13:12 states the USA will make the world follow the Papacy, it seems clear that such a bill passed by the US government would quickly be adopted by governments worldwide. In this way, people could be identified by their adherence to the law, rather than receiving a literal mark.

The placing of the mark on either the right hand or the forehead would then be symbolic of why people choose to take up the practice. Those marked on the forehead, are those who have given thought to the act of worshiping on Sunday; they believe it is right, and make a decision to carry it out. Whilst those marked on their right hands, are those who remain unconvinced of its veracity, but are fearful of the penalty for refusal - a death sentence. Therefore, they carry out the action without belief. This seems a feasible explanation, when we compare it with the people who receive the seal of God. We have already met these people in Revelation chapter seven.

God's people only receive His seal on their foreheads, none will receive it on their hands. This signifies that all who are saved will have made a conscious decision to accept the salvation that comes only through Jesus Christ. None will be saved without this belief. If the mark of the beast is a literal, indelible mark that must be stamped on (or injected into) billions of people's heads or hands, then the seal of God must also be a literal mark. However, Revelation 7:3 states it is the angels of God who seal God's people in their foreheads. Clearly, the decision to follow Jesus and His teachings allow His people to be symbolically marked. Therefore, we can safely conclude that the seal of God is symbolic of adherence to the dictates of God and His law, and the mark of the beast symbolises adherence to the dictates of the Catholic Church, which boasts of instituting a law in opposition to God.

Revelation makes it clear that at the end of time only two groups of people will exist; those who have the mark of the beast, and those who have the seal of God. There will be no fence sitters; everyone will have decided to whom they give their allegiance. This will not be an easy time for God's people. Revelation 13:17 tells us they will be prevented from buying or selling; even life's basic necessities are denied them. No doubt, they will be forced to go into hiding, for they will be under the threat of death. It is the image of the beast, the USA Protestant movement that, in alliance with the government, institutes and enforces this persecution of God's people. It will act on behalf of the Catholic Church that, in turn, is controlled by the devil himself: the Unholy Trinity working in unison to deceive the world.

Remember, the symbolic mark of the beast is identified as *"the name of the beast or the number of its name"* (Revelation 13:17). We already know the name of the beast is the Roman Catholic Church, but is there a special name associated with the Papacy, and a number that goes with this name?

Revelation 13:18 – answers the question. We are told the leopard-like beast can be identified as a number, which can be calculated. It is a number of a man, which is the number of his name: the number is 666. We are also told we will need wisdom and insight to calculate this number. Therefore, we must look for a special man, with a special name, who represents the Roman Catholic Church and whose name can be calculated as the number 666.

As we already know, there are many significant numbers in the book of Revelation. We have already seen lots of sevens and twelves, significant of perfection or spiritual completeness. The number six is also significant. To the Jews, the number six denotes evil, for it signifies missing the mark, or falling short of perfection (7). Therefore 666 represents extreme evil.

There is a man who represents the Papacy. We know him as the Pope. I must add here, this does not apply to any specific Pope, but to the Pope's role as Pontiff, the head of the Catholic Church. The Pope is the church's figurehead, and symbol of all the church stands for.

The Pope wears a mitre, and around the mitre there is a Latin insignia, which reads:

VICARIUS FILII DEI

This means 'Vicar of the Son of God'. The title itself is blasphemous, because the Vicar of the Son of God, in other words, Jesus' representative on earth, is not the Pope. It is the Holy Spirit (see John 14:26 and John 16:7-15). By taking this title, the Pope is designating himself as God on earth; a representation of the Son of God. This is certainly an attempt to counterfeit the identity of Jesus.

The name **Vicarius Filii Dei** can be calculated as a number when expressed as Roman numerals, as follows:

V	5
I	1
C	100
A	0
R	0
I	1
U	5
S	0
Total	112

F	0
I	1
L	50
I	1
I	1
Total	53

D	500
E	0
I	1
Total	501

Grand Total - 666

Whilst other famous historical figures may also have names that, when expressed as Roman numerals, add up to 666, none of them have all the beast's characteristics. Nor do their lives fulfil the required historical facts, events and actions that make up the profile of the leopard-like beast of Revelation 13. We are given numerous identifiers as to who this beast is. Therefore, with all the evidence presented in this prophecy, we can confidently state the following:

- In its end time form, the first beast (the leopard-like beast) of Revelation 13 is the Papacy;
- The Papacy is represented by a man (the Pope) who can be identified by the number 666;
- The second beast (the lamb-like beast) of Revelation 13 is the USA;
- The USA will make an image to Catholicism: the image is a false Protestant movement;
- This false religion, that is affiliated to the USA State or government, will institute a law which is a defining mark of the Catholic Church (this mark is Sunday worship);
- The law will decree that all people must worship on Sunday. If they refuse, they will be prevented from buying or selling, and sentenced to death.

Revelation Chapter Fourteen

THE THREE ANGELS' MESSAGES

Based on Revelation 14:1-20

It would be understandable, if we found John feeling a little perturbed at this point: he has just witnessed a counterfeit Holy Trinity led by the devil, successfully deceiving the entire world. Consequently, those who defy the dictates of evil-inspired governments are labelled as outlaws, and stripped of their right to carry out financial transactions. They are now eligible only for arrest and death.

John must have marvelled at the phenomenon of history repeating itself. For here he is in the first century AD, a man in his 90s, imprisoned on the Isle of Patmos, tortured and sentenced to hard labour, all because he has dared to preach the gospel of Jesus Christ. And now he knows that at the end of time, the devil will not have altered his tactics, his insatiable desire to destroy God's church will not have diminished; he will still be inciting men to rid the earth of those who maintain loyalty to the word of God.

But, here comes some encouragement.

The first vision of Revelation chapter fourteen confirms the victory of the saints of God.

Revelation 14:1 – The vision jumps forward in time. John sees the Lamb, Jesus Christ, standing on Mount Zion. This is not the earthly Mount Zion situated in Jerusalem. Hebrews 12:22 makes it clear that when Jesus collects His people from the earth at His second coming, He gathers them to the heavenly Mount Zion where God dwells. Thus, John is viewing Jesus in heaven, and with Him are the 144,000 whom we first met in Revelation 7. At that time, they were living on earth at the end of time. They were about to receive the seal of God, which would equip them to endure the great Time of Trouble coming on the earth. In Revelation 13 we saw the terrible Time of Trouble.

Now, we see the 144,000 victorious in heaven. They have the seal of God on their foreheads, which is identified as the name of Jesus, and the name of His Father. Here is confirmation, the 144,000 have made it. Despite all the persecution the devil could throw at them; they have made it to heaven.

Let us once again take a look at the seal of God. As explained in chapter 7, having the names of Jesus and the Father written on the forehead is symbolic of an acceptance of Jesus in the life, that leads us to follow God's principles. It is the sign of a love relationship with the Godhead. We symbolically receive this seal on our foreheads because we must make a cognitive choice to enter into this relationship; we must decide to follow Jesus.

At the end of time, there will be only two classes on earth; those with the seal of God, and those with the mark of the beast. As we have seen in Revelation 13, the mark of the beast can be received either on the forehead or the right hand; for some will have decided to worship the beast, while others will follow the beast out of fear of the death penalty. This second group know the truth, but will assent to the lie in order to save their lives. And, just as all who follow the leopard-like beast will signify their allegiance by worshiping on the beast's day (Sunday), so those with the seal of God will signify their choice to follow Jesus by worshiping on the day instituted by God at creation (the Seventh-day Sabbath, Saturday) (see Genesis 2:1-3).

Neither the mark of the beast, nor the seal of God are literal marks. The day on which you choose to worship will reveal whose mark you bear, and to whom you belong.

Revelation 14:2-3 – John views the heavenly scene, and next hears heaven's orchestra tuning up, like the roar of rushing waters and a peal of thunder. It is the musical intro to a new song that can only be sung by the 144,000. The holy angels are present, as are the four Cherubim, and the twenty-four elders. They stand before the throne of God, but remain silent, for the song concerns an experience they have not shared. It is the song of how the 144,000 withstood the Time of Trouble, and were redeemed from the earth.

Revelation 14:4-5 – tell us some of the words of the song. It describes the 144,000 as people who did not defile themselves with women, but are virgins. As the 144,000 will be made up of both men and women, this must be symbolic language. If we look at the prophetic symbols here, we understand that in Bible prophecy a woman is the symbol for a church (see Ephesians 5:25-27). The people of God who remain virgins; undefiled by women, are a church that has kept faithful to Jesus, her Husband, and not defiled herself with the false doctrines of other churches.

The song goes on to say, the 144,000 follow the Lamb wherever He goes. That is, they are not deceived by the counterfeit Christ. They follow no-one but Jesus, and adhere only to His teachings. The 144,000 have remained true to Jesus. He has purchased them from among mankind using the currency of His blood shed at Calvary. In other words, He saved them. They are described as *"firstfruits"*.

Ancient Israel was instructed by God to give a small offering from the first harvest of their crops as an act of thanksgiving. The offering of firstfruits was a guarantee that the larger offering would be made (see Deuteronomy 26:1-11). Therefore, the 144,000 are called firstfruits; for, they stand before the throne of God, as evidence of the salvation of all those who through the ages have remained faithful to God.

The song then says, no lie is found in the mouths of the 144,000; they are blameless. How wonderful that men and women who once followed the dictates of their sinful, selfish natures, can now be called blameless. This is only possible because they have given themselves to Jesus, and He has covered them with His own righteous character. They have been washed and made clean in the blood of the Lamb (see 1 Corinthians 6:9-11).

Now that John has seen the ultimate fate of the 144,000, he can breathe a sigh of relief; a happy ending is assured.

John is now taken back to earth, to a time before the Time of Trouble, when God's people are instructed to give the gospel message to the world, and warn of the troubled times to come. This message is commonly known as The Three Angels' Messages.

In Revelation chapter ten, we learned that the 19th century Adventists, who did not lose their faith despite the Great Disappointment, clung to the instruction given in Revelation 10:11 *"You must prophecy again about many peoples, nations, languages and kings."* They took this instruction to heart and looked for the special message they were to preach. They found the message in Revelation 14:6-12 - The Three Angels' Messages. Through their study of the prophecies of Daniel, the Adventists realised they were in the time of the end. Therefore, the final gospel message for humankind must be preached to the world, and then Jesus would come (see Matthew 24:14).

Revelation 14:6-7 – John sees the first angel flying in mid-air, with the eternal gospel, to be proclaimed to everyone on earth – *"every nation, tribe, language and people"*.

In the early chapters of Revelation, we discovered that angels (Greek 'angelos') are messengers of God, and can refer to heavenly or earthly messengers. As this messenger is proclaiming the eternal gospel to humanity, we know the angel symbolises earthly messengers; as it is the work of mankind to preach the gospel (see Matthew 28:18-20, Acts 1:8).

The message is announced in mid-air, showing its universality – it is for everyone, and must reach all nations of the earth, no-one is excluded.

The proclamation is called the eternal gospel. In other words, it is the good news of salvation; namely, that Jesus came and died so that every human being can be saved from eternal death, and instead, gain eternal life (see John 3:16). This gospel has not changed. From the beginning when Adam and Eve sinned, God promised a Saviour would come to reconcile humankind to God (see Genesis 3:15). The final message to mankind is the same good news, for it is only through the life, death and resurrection of Jesus that anyone can be saved – there is no other way (see Acts 4:11,12).

We are told the messenger has a loud voice. It is clear this message is to be proclaimed openly for everyone to hear. And the special message is:

"Fear God and give Him glory, because the hour of His judgement has come. Worship Him who made the heavens, the earth, the sea and the springs of water." (Revelation 14:6,7)

Surely, this is a call for humankind to return to the worship of the Creator of the universe. It is fitting that the message goes out to the people living at the end of time, for we are the generation that has embraced Evolution, Atheism, Humanism, Pantheism, Mysticism, Spiritism and Satanism. Indeed, since the end time began in 1798 following the Dark Ages, a plethora of new theories opposing the existence of God has flooded our societies, our families, our schools, our literature, and our media. It is unfashionable to believe in Creation, and a God who sustains the universe. Little wonder God's end time message to the planet is 'Remember I exist. I have always existed. I am still here and I still want to save you.'

It is interesting that the wording of the First Angel's Message is very like one of the commandments.

Revelation 14:7 calls us to *"Worship Him who made the heavens, the earth, the sea and the springs of water."* It reminds us of God's instruction in the fourth commandment which calls us to worship the Lord on the Sabbath day because

He *"made the heavens and the earth, the sea and all that is in them . . ."* (see Exodus 20:8-11).

God wants us to remember Him, who He is, and what He has done. He reminds us He is the God who gave us the Ten Commandments. He is the only one we should worship. And indeed, He is the only one who can save us. Those who remember who God is, by keeping holy His Sabbath day, are the ones who receive the seal of God on their foreheads, and who make it successfully through the time of great tribulation. They are the ones who stand victorious with Jesus on Mount Zion in heaven. This, therefore, is a love message from God. He wants mankind to come back to Him and be saved. Moreover, Revelation 14:7 tells us we should *"Fear God and give Him glory because the hour of His judgement has come."*

To *"fear God and give Him glory"* is to love and revere Him; to approach Him with awe and wonder; to glorify Him; for after all, He is our Creator and Redeemer. But maybe too, our reverence should include an element of fear, for He is also our Judge.

We learned from Revelation 10 that those who lived through the Great Disappointment finally realised 22 October 1844 was not the date of the Second Advent, but the day when Jesus would enter the Most Holy Place of the heavenly temple, there to begin the Investigative Judgement. Since that date, judgement has been going on in heaven, and unfortunately, the majority of people alive today are oblivious to this fact. The commonly held belief that when Jesus comes, judgement will take place at that time, is a myth not borne out by the Bible. When Jesus comes the second time, the judgement that decides who will make it to heaven, will already have taken place. Jesus will be coming with His pre-determined rewards (see Revelation 22:12). People need to know that while they are getting on with life here and now, a heavenly court is in session, determining the fate of souls. This is the most important news for the world today; a message that should certainly be proclaimed with a loud voice.

Summary of the First Angel's Message:

God is calling humanity back to the worship of the true God and Creator of the Universe, for He is the only one who can save us from eternal death. And, time is running out. Those who accept the invitation will worship God on the true Sabbath (the seventh day of the week). It is imperative that we accept this invitation as mankind is presently being judged by God, and Jesus is soon to come.

Revelation 14:8 – The Second Angel's Message is for our information:

"Fallen! Fallen is Babylon the Great, which made all the nations drink the maddening wine of her adulteries."

Who is Babylon the Great, and what does it mean that she is fallen?

The name Babylon comes from the word Babel, first seen in the story of the Tower of Babel (see Genesis 11:1-9). The city where the tower was built was called Babel because this is where God confused the speech of the builders. Babel means confusion.

Later, in the book of Daniel, we see the Jews captured by the idol worshiping Babylonians, and kept in captivity for 70 years. Babylon was overthrown by the Persians in 539BC, who then largely destroyed it in 480BC.

As Revelation 14:8 is a prophecy for the end of time just before Jesus returns, it cannot be referring to the ancient city of Babel nor to the world ruling nation, as neither now exist. This message forms part of the last global gospel announcement.

We must remember that we are dealing with Bible prophecy here, and we already know that a prophetic woman symbolises a church. In Revelation 14:8, Babylon is the name of a woman. Therefore, we are looking at a church. The name Babylon is significant, for the church has the same characteristics as the

174

ancient town of Babel, and the historical Babylonian nation; it promotes confused doctrine and false worship.

We saw God's church depicted as a virtuous woman in Revelation chapter twelve. However, Babylon, the church of Revelation 14:8, is not virtuous. She was once the true church but now she is its antithesis. This church is fallen. Just as we talk about fallen women, we also have fallen churches. Babylon has fallen away from the truth; it preaches confused, false doctrine. It must be avoided at all costs, for it is fallen not once, but twice. It fell during the reign of Pagan Rome when Emperor Constantine compromised Christianity with Pagan practices. And, it will fall again when the Protestant movements, formed during the 16th Century Reformation, re-join the apostate church, and begin to act in unison with its false teachings. Surely, we are seeing this happen in our time. Here is a quotation from 'The Guardian Newspaper' - 31 October 2017:

"Catholic and Protestant leaders have stressed their mutual bonds 500 years after the start of the Reformation, a movement that tore apart western Christianity and sparked a string of bloody religious wars in Europe lasting more than a century.

"A service in Westminster Abbey on Tuesday marked the anniversary of the date in 1517 on which the German theologian Martin Luther submitted The 95 Theses to the archbishop of Mainz, as well as nailing a copy to the door of a church in Wittenberg, lighting the fuse of the Reformation.

"The archbishop of Canterbury, Justin Welby, presented a text by the Anglican communion affirming a joint declaration by the Roman Catholic church and global Protestant bodies, described as 'a sign of healing after 500 years of division'."

Remember, earlier in Revelation 14, we saw the triumphant 144,000, redeemed from the earth. Part of their song celebrated their non-defilement with women. In other words, they had not been deceived by false churches with confused doctrine. They remained faithful to Jesus and had therefore gained the victory.

We are told that Babylon is *"Great"*. This is not a small, insignificant movement. She operates on a grand scale; known by everyone and worshiped by the world. She makes *". . .all the nations drink the maddening wine of her adulteries."* (Revelation 14:8). This church's confused doctrines make people mad, just as wine makes people drunk. The church is an adulteress because she is not faithful to the truth of God. She plays around with false beliefs; mixes up the truths of the Bible. The people who listen to her become confused and maddened.

We will come across this false church, Babylon, time and time again. It is apostate religion through the ages, and includes every church not following the teachings of God as written in the Bible. Babylon will become increasingly prominent at the end of time. We will get to know her well.

Summary of The Second Angel's Message:

Stay away from the worldwide apostate religions that will unite and become prominent in the end time. The movement appears great, but actually, it has massively fallen away from the truth. If you take on its doctrines, you will become confused and maddened, unable to distinguish truth from error.

Revelation 14:9-11 – The Third Angel's Message is a warning:

"If anyone worships the beast and its image and receives its mark on their forehead or on their hand, they, too, will drink the wine of God's fury, which is poured full strength into the cup of His wrath . . ."

This message should be more familiar to us as we have come across much of its language before. It refers to the leopard-like beast of Revelation 13 that has an image. Its mark is placed on either the forehead or right hand of its followers. We have already identified this beast as the Papal power, and its mark of authority as worshiping on Sunday, the first day of the week.

In Revelation 13 it appeared that those with the mark of the beast had the upper hand, but now we are told they are specifically designated to drink more wine, but this is not the wine of Babylon that confuses and maddens. This time, it is God who is furious. Anyone who drinks God's wine will experience His fury, full strength. They are the ones who persecuted God's people by hounding them, imprisoning them, forbidding them to buy or sell, sentencing them to death. Now God wreaks vengeance on the people who have the beast's mark. He holds nothing back. In the Third Angel's Message, we are warned, for God does not want any of us to suffer His wrath. The message is, 'Don't receive the mark of the beast!'

The remainder of the Third Angel's Message needs some interpretation for it has generally been misunderstood. It says:

". . . They will be tormented with burning sulphur in the presence of the holy angels and of the Lamb. And the smoke of their torment will rise for ever and ever. There will be no rest day or night for those who worship the beast and its image, or for anyone who receives the mark of its name." (Revelation 14:10-11)

Traditionally, these verses have been used to justify the false doctrine of an eternal hell, where people burn throughout eternity. However, the Bible does not support this teaching.

Let us separate the truth from the error. It is true that those who have tormented God's people; persecuted and tortured them, will themselves receive torment in hell fire, but they will not burn forever. Revelation 22:12 says the wicked will receive punishment according to what they have done. That is, those people designated as wicked, will suffer in the fire for as long as their particular sins warrant; which means, their torment will come to an end. And indeed, it would be unfair for, say, mass murderers to receive the same

177

punishment as those who have been less wicked. Therefore, even in meting out punishment, God is just. Each person is punished proportionately.

Jude 7 tells us that the destruction by fire of Sodom and Gomorrah serves as an example of those who will suffer in the final hell fire (which it calls *"eternal"* fire). Therefore, as Sodom and Gomorrah are not still burning today (the fire eventually went out once the cities were destroyed), it appears that 'eternal' refers to the effects of the fire. In other words, the burning will exist as long as is necessary to complete its work. However, the effects will be eternal. Just as Sodom and Gomorrah were never rebuilt, so no-one will come back to life from hell fire.

This understanding is confirmed in Malachi 4:1-3:

"Surely the day is coming; it will burn like a furnace. All the arrogant and every evildoer will be stubble, and the day that is coming will set them on fire, says the Lord Almighty. Not a root or a branch will be left of them . . . they will be ashes under the soles of your feet on the day when I act, says the Lord Almighty."

This clearly tells us, people will not be burning in hell fire forever. In fact, hell fire will not only destroy the wicked people, it will also cleanse the earth. Therefore, hell fire will take place on the earth. When it has completed its work, a new earth will emerge on which the righteous people will live throughout eternity (see Revelation 21:1). That is why Malachi speaks about God's people walking on the site where the fire has burned (but more of this later).

In Revelation 14:11 we are told, it is the smoke of the fire that rises *"for ever and ever"*, signifying the eternal consequences of this executionary act. No-one will return to life from this death: the people thrown into the fire will get no rest from their punishment, for they will burn and perish.

(We will study more about the nature of hell fire in Revelation chapter twenty.)

Summary of the Third Angel's Message:

Those who follow the dictates of the Roman Catholic Church, or the false Protestant Church, set up by the USA, and choose to worship on the first day of the week (Sunday), will finally be thrown into hell fire, and burned up in accordance with their wicked deeds.

Revelation 14:12 – Those who experienced the Great Disappointment of 1844, and began preaching the end time gospel messages, have now died. The work has been passed to us, and we are to preach with a loud voice. This is not a job for the faint-hearted. The messages will not be popular. It will take courage, but we must preach them. Jesus will not come until the whole world is aware that:

- God is our Creator and worthy of our worship;
- The Investigative Judgement is taking place NOW;
- We must follow what the Bible says, and stay away from false, confused doctrine preached by apostate churches;
- We must not make Sunday our day of worship, for by doing so, we will receive the mark of the beast, which leads to hell fire, the final death.

Therefore, we must preach with patient endurance, not becoming discouraged, when our efforts appear of no avail. Whatever the reception, God's people are to continue preaching the Three Angels' Messages. This is their most important work.

At this most serious time in earth's history the true church is identified as those who keep the commandments of God (all ten), and remain faithful to Jesus; they do not deviate from His teachings. This is the end time church, the remnant of the church of Revelation 12. Anyone wishing to find the true church of God on earth today should look for a church with these characteristics.

Revelation 14:13 – John then hears the voice of the Holy Spirit telling him to write the following:

"Blessed are the dead who die in the Lord from now on . . . they will rest from their labour, for their deeds will follow them."

Unlike the wicked people who end up in hell fire, to die without respite, those who are faithful to God, and die before Jesus comes, will find rest from their arduous lives. Remember, many of them were persecuted for their faith. Now they can rest in their graves, safe in the knowledge that their good deeds will bear testimony on their behalf, when they are judged by God.

This would have been comforting news to John, who, now at the end of his long life, knowing from the visions received that there was much to happen before Jesus returned, could be at peace, assured that although he would be laid to rest, all that he had done for the spreading of the gospel would be remembered in the judgement.

Moreover, those who had faithfully begun the preaching of The Three Angels' Messages, but would not live to see Jesus return, could rest, knowing their contribution to the evangelising of the world would not be forgotten.

Now that we have learned of The Three Angels' Messages; the last preaching of the gospel to the world, the scene changes.

The Two Harvests

Revelation 14:14 – Once again we jump forward in time. The Three Angels' Messages have been preached, and every man's (and woman's) case has been decided. John is now shown a vision of the figurative separation of the righteous and the wicked. He witnesses two harvests, based on the Palestinian agricultural year: the grain harvest beginning with barley and ending with wheat in July, and the fruit harvest beginning with grapes in late summer.

John sees Jesus wearing a golden crown of victory, pronouncing His divine rulership. He is sitting on a cloud and holding a sharp sickle.

Revelation 14:15 – An angel flies out of the heavenly temple and shouts to Jesus, *"Take your sickle and reap, because the time to reap has come, for the harvest of the earth is ripe."*

Revelation 14:16 – Jesus swings His sickle over the earth and it is harvested.

Revelation 14:17-18 – John then sees a second harvest conducted by an angel. The angel flies out of the temple carrying a sharp sickle, and is followed by a second angel, who has charge of the fire from the temple altar. Perhaps this signifies the type of death allotted to those who have chosen not to be saved.

The angel shouts to the one with the sickle, *"Take your sharp sickle and gather the clusters of grapes from the earth's vine, because its grapes are ripe."*

Revelation 14:19-20 – The angel dutifully swings his sickle over the earth, gathers the grapes and throws them into the great winepress of God's wrath. We are then told the grapes are trampled in the winepress outside the city. But instead of grape juice being produced, out flows blood, rising as high as the horses' bridles for a distance of 200 miles.

This vision is a representation of the reward of the righteous, and the punishment of the wicked. So what lessons are we to draw from this?

First, there will be two harvests: one for the righteous and one for the wicked. The harvest of the righteous (the wheat) will be conducted by Jesus, signifying Jesus gathering the saints at His second coming (see 1 Thessalonians 4:15-17). This picture fits with the parable of the wheat and tares (see Matthew 13:24-30), in which God's people, signified by wheat, are harvested at the end of time.

The second harvest, conducted by an angel, is of the wicked, and leads to the death of a vast amount of people. Unfortunately, it appears the number destroyed in hell fire far outweighs the number of the saved (see Matthew 7:13,14).

Another interesting point is that the winepress into which the unrighteous grapes are thrown is located outside the city; and as we will see in Revelation chapter twenty, the wicked will indeed die outside the New Jerusalem.

The conclusion of Revelation 14 shows that once the messages of the three angels have been preached to the world, each individual will be fully equipped to make a decision either for, or against, Jesus and their own salvation. The two harvests show the consequences of their decision.

Both harvests take place when the earth is ripe. Thus, God will not allow the earth to be harvested until all inhabitants have heard the gospel and made their final decision.

Whilst there is time, we should all be deciding whom we will serve.

Why would anyone choose to die in the second harvest?

Revelation Chapter Fifteen

PREPARATION FOR THE SEVEN LAST PLAGUES

Based on Revelation 15:1-8

In Revelation 14, we saw the final preaching of the gospel message to the world. This is set in our present. We then saw the population of earth separated into two harvests – the harvest of the righteous, and the harvest of the wicked. These figurative harvests take place as a result of The Three Angels' Messages being preached, for it enables everyone on earth to choose whether to be saved, or not. In Revelation 15 we move to our near future, when the decision regarding who is saved, and who is lost, has been made. God's people have now been sealed, and the four winds held by the avenging angels are released. There is nothing to stop God's judgements coming upon the people who have persecuted the righteous during the Time of Trouble. Now we are ready for the Seven Last Plagues; the beginning of God's retribution.

In Revelation 15 we see preparation in heaven for the Seven Last Plagues. And, Revelation 16 describes the plagues themselves, unleashed on the wicked people living on the earth just before Christ's second coming.

Revelation 15:1 – John sees, what he calls a *"great and marvellous sign"*; the seven angels designated to pour out the *"Seven Last Plagues"*. John tells us, God's judgements are aptly named because *"with them God's wrath is completed."* In other words, these are the last plagues God will use to punish humankind. They will be terrible; for God's anger will be poured out in full measure on those who have sought to harm His people. We already know the number seven is symbolic of perfection or completeness. The Seven Last Plagues are God's perfect and complete answer to those who have resisted His every invitation, followed the beast, chosen to continue in their evil ways, and refused to repent. They must now suffer the consequences of their choices.

The plagues also answer the questions we often ask when suffering, violence, untimely deaths, crime, injustice and even natural disasters occur – 'Why does God allow this to happen?' 'Why doesn't He intervene?' 2 Peter 3:9 tells us God is merciful. He has allowed time to continue because He is giving humanity time to repent and take advantage of salvation. He is waiting for as many as possible to be saved. He is loath to wrap everything up while there are people still deciding whether to follow Him or not. He will wait until the last person who can be saved, is saved. He has therefore allowed the prolonging of time. Unfortunately, while He waits for people to repent, evil men are becoming more evil, and demonstrating the character of the devil.

When considering these big questions, it is also appropriate to consider the matter of our being free moral agents. When God created humankind, He gave them the greatest gift possible – freedom of choice. He allowed us to choose to do good, or evil. And, despite Adam and Eve's choice to disobey Him, God has never taken the power of choice from us. This means, He will allow men and women to choose to harm themselves, and each other; to make despicable moral choices; to destroy their environment, in fact, to do anything imaginable. How painful it must be for God to witness His creation acting out their very worst conceptions. That is why Jesus came; to demonstrate a better way; to bring us back to the image of God; and show us that we can choose to do good and behave in accordance with His principles; showing love to God, and to our fellow man. God intervened in the most powerful of ways; He sent His only Son to live among us, and die instead of us, so that we could live a life in harmony with our Creator. Jesus spent most of His time on earth helping the needy; He healed the sick; raised the dead; fed the hungry; gave hope to the downtrodden and marginalised of society. His attitude to his fellows showed the same attitude our heavenly Father shows to mankind (see Psalm 146:6-9).

The atrocities that plague our planet come about largely through our own choices. However, we can be thankful God does not leave us alone to deal with the consequences. The devil has brought our world to the brink of destruction many times. He stands behind humankind inspiring their evil actions, and causing natural disasters. But, as long as time lasts, God is continually working with us, sustaining life and intervening in the affairs of men in order to keep our planet in existence. The devil would have destroyed the earth long ago but for the preserving power of our Creator.

However, as soon as the number of the saved is made up, and God's people have been sealed, Jesus will stand up. He will come out of the Most Holy Place in heaven, and the Investigative Judgement will be pronounced closed (see Daniel 12:1). God will then give the order to the four angels of Revelation 7 to loose the winds of strife. His protection will be removed from the earth. Now the wicked can be punished.

Revelation 15:2-4 - Before the plagues fall, John is once again given a view of God's people in heaven. This is a flash-forward to God's people triumphant. They stand on the sea of glass before the throne of God. They have been victorious over the beast (the Papacy), the image of the beast (false Protestantism), and over the number of the beast's name (666). All this refers to Revelation 13:11-18, which describes how the USA government will institute a law forbidding religious worship on any day other than Sunday, and persecute all those who choose to obey the law of God and worship on the seventh-day Sabbath. This will lead to a great Time of Trouble for God's people who refuse to worship the beast, or its image. And of course, we recognise the beast by the number 666, which identifies it as the Papacy.

At the time before Jesus comes, when the Seven Last Plagues fall on the earth, God's people are still living here. They have not, as some believe, been taken to heaven in a secret rapture. They must endure the plagues, but will not be harmed by them. To encourage them, God shows them a picture. They see themselves in heaven receiving eternal life. God is saying to His children, 'Things are bad, I know, but you will be victorious. Visualise it. Believe it.'

Here is the vision. In heaven, we are once again shown the sea of glass, described as glowing with fire. We already know from Revelation chapter four that the sea of glass is situated before the throne of God. So, anyone who reaches the sea of glass, knows they are saved.

Standing by the sea are the 144,000 (God's people who live to witness the Second Advent. They are the ones who have experienced the Time of Trouble). Harps are given to them by God Himself, and without rehearsal, they sing the song of Moses and the Lamb. Of course, the Lamb is Jesus. We can understand why their song celebrates Him. It is a song of salvation; gratitude to God for the Lamb who takes away the sin of the world (John 1:29). He is our Redeemer, and it is only through our relationship with Him that we are saved. But, why is their song also connected with Moses? We see the song of Moses in Exodus 15:1-18. The Children of Israel sang this after being delivered from Pharaoh and his army through the parting of the Red Sea. It is a song of deliverance. This will also be the experience of the 144,000. During the Time of Trouble, seemingly, they were at the mercy of their enemies, but God delivered them, and now they identify with the experience of Moses.

Here are the words of that special song:
> "Great and marvellous are your deeds,
> Lord God Almighty.
> Just and true are your ways,
> King of the nations.
> Who will not fear you, Lord
> and bring glory to your name?
> For you alone are holy.
> All nations will come
> and worship before you,
> for your righteous acts have been revealed."
(Revelation 15:3,4)

186

Revelation 15:5-8 - Once again, John is shown the temple in heaven. He sees the Ten Commandments kept there. Their presence signifies the importance of God's law. The law has not been abolished, as some believe. Its precepts are still binding on humanity. Moreover, those who have set it aside with disdain are about to be punished (see Matthew 5:17-19). John notices the way into the temple is open, and, from the temple come the seven angels who will pour out the Seven Last Plagues. They are wearing robes of clean, shining linen, with golden sashes around their chests.

There is no doubt these plagues are from God. One of the Cherubim gives a golden bowl to each angel. Each bowl is filled with a plague described as *"the wrath of God"*.

Then the temple is filled with smoke, so no-one can enter until the plagues have been poured out. Up until now, the heavenly temple has been a hive of activity. When Jesus ascended to heaven at the end of His time on earth, He became our Intercessor in the Holy Place. Then, since 1844 the Investigative Judgement has been taking place in the Most Holy Place, and Jesus has been mediating for the righteous before the throne of God. In Revelation 15, we see the time when this work is completed. God's people have had their names retained in the Book of Life, and they have been sealed. Now, no-one is allowed to enter the temple; all activity is transferred to earth. God's people must survive through the time of the Seven Last Plagues without a Mediator. Nevertheless, we must not worry, for the saints are sealed. They are protected from His plagues.

Revelation Chapter Sixteen

THE SEVEN LAST PLAGUES

Based on Revelation 16:1-21

God will pour out the Seven Last Plagues on the earth to punish the wicked for their evil deeds. This will happen during the period just before the second coming of Christ. At this time, the fate of the righteous still living on earth will be secure. Having been found not guilty in the Investigative Judgement, their salvation is guaranteed; they will be safe from the temptations of the devil; and no longer able to sin. However, as Jesus has left the Most Holy Place in the heavenly temple, His people must live through this terrible time without their heavenly Mediator. Whilst the wicked will suffer physical torment from the plagues, the righteous will suffer mental anguish. For despite the assurance that they have been faithful to Jesus and, therefore, must be saved, they will recall their past sins and distrust their own characters, grappling with the thought that nevertheless they may still be unworthy of heaven.

This is not the first time God has used plagues to punish the earth. Exodus chapters seven to eleven tell of ten plagues He unleashed on Egypt, in order to convince Pharaoh to free the Children of Israel from slavery, and allow them to leave the country. Pharaoh had defied God by oppressing and torturing His chosen people. He had set himself up against the God of heaven. And, although warned by Moses not to take this stance, and the consequences of opposing the Creator of the universe, Pharaoh chose not to listen. His attitude was unyielding, and his stubborn defiance increased. Therefore, God brought on Egypt His promised judgements. The ten plagues affected the Egyptian people, their livestock and their land. Indeed, the country was brought to utter ruin and its people to abject misery before Pharaoh let the Israelites leave. All of which, could have been avoided if Pharaoh had listened to God and humbled his defiant nature.

And, so it will be with the people living just before the coming of Jesus. They have received ample warning to turn from their rebellious ways; to accept Jesus, and be saved. However, they have consistently rejected the gospel of salvation, followed the devil, and finally engaged in his schemes to destroy those who faithfully keep God's commandments. Now God will bring about all that He has promised. The Seven Last Plagues will fall. Consequently, much of the earth will be ruined, and the people will suffer abject misery. We will see much of the plagues of Egypt repeated in the Seven Last Plagues.

Revelation 16:1 - John hears a command from heaven to the seven angels, instructing them to pour out the Seven Last Plagues on the earth.

Some readers of Revelation have questioned whether the Seven Last Plagues are literal events, and indeed, we have continually reminded ourselves that Revelation is a symbolic book. However, as with the Seven Seals and Seven Trumpets in Revelation chapters 6-11, the events, whilst pictured through symbols, did actually happen. Also, we can take our lead from the fact that the Seven Last Plagues mirror the ten literal plagues of Egypt.

We will find that the Seven Last Plagues will follow the precedence of the Seven Seals and Seven Trumpets; they will be literal events pictured symbolically as angels pouring out bowls on the earth.

Revelation 16:2 – The First Plague is poured out on the land, and ugly, festering sores immediately break out on the people who have the mark of the beast, and worship its image. A mark for a mark. Although the mark of the beast is not a physical mark but is shown through the practice of worshiping on the first day of the week instead of the seventh day, at this stage, God marks those who follow the beast with rotting boils. Those with the mark of the beast are marked by God.

Revelation 16:3 – The Second Plague is poured out on the sea, which straight away turns to blood and everything in it dies. This, of course will affect a great amount of the world's food supply. Moreover, international transport and travel by sea will be halted. There also appears to be a link here with international trade, and the way the false churches have been fostering trade relations with the rulers of the earth. (We will examine this again in Revelation chapter eighteen when we see commerce disrupted.)

Revelation 16:4-7 – The Third Plague is poured on the rivers, and springs (in other words, drinking water), which also turn to blood. The angel explains the significance of this plague, for he says:

"You are just in these judgements, O Holy One,
You who are and were;
for they have shed the blood of your holy people and your prophets, and you
have given them blood to drink as they deserve."

In Revelation 6:10 the souls of the martyred saints under the altar cried out *"How long, Sovereign Lord… until you judge the inhabitants of the earth and avenge our blood?"* Now God keeps His promise. He brings retribution by giving the wicked blood to drink. And the altar in heaven responds with:

"Yes, Lord God Almighty,
True and just are your judgements" (Revelation 16:7)

Heaven is satisfied.

Revelation 16:8 – The Fourth Plague is poured on the sun, which is now allowed to scorch people. The practices of humanity have been eroding the earth's atmosphere for decades. Now this plague completes the work man has begun. In addition, this will adversely affect the world's food supply, as all plant life is dried up (see Joel 1:10-12).

The fourth plague has significance for those who, inadvertently, have compelled worship of the pagan sun god. They have enforced worship on Sunday, and now the sun scorches them with unfiltered heat.

Revelation 16:9 - We are told that although the people are seared by the intense heat of the sun, they continue to curse the name of God, and refuse to repent and worship Him. This is further proof of the nature of those who have rejected salvation; they are fixed in their decision and nothing will change their minds. They refuse to take responsibility for the evil deeds they have committed, and instead blame God, with curses, for the punishment they now receive.

Revelation 16:10-11 – The Fifth Plague is poured out on the throne of the beast, which plunges its kingdom into darkness. We have already learned in Revelation 13, that the beast is the Papal power, which persecutes the people of God, and sets itself up as a counterfeit Christ. Just as Jesus has a throne, so His counterfeit has a throne. This could be the Vatican City, in Rome, where the Pope resides. But wherever it is, the darkness that envelopes it will be of such intensity that it causes people to gnaw their tongues in agony. And, once again, they curse the God of heaven because of their pain and sores, and refuse to repent of what they have done. It appears then, that at the time of the fifth plague, people are still suffering from the boils of the first plague.

The Papal power is unmasked; this physical darkness, that causes such agony, is no doubt symbolic of the spiritual darkness created by the Roman Catholic Church throughout history. It deceived the world and turned men away from the truth, whilst purporting to speak for God.

Revelation 16:12 – **The Sixth Plague** is poured on the great river Euphrates, and its water is dried up to prepare the way for the Kings from the East.

This plague will be further amplified when we look at Revelation chapter seventeen, but at this point, we can look at the symbolism used. Remember, the Seven Last Plagues fall in the period just before Jesus returns to earth. And, as Matthew 24:27 tells us that Jesus' coming will be like the " . . . *lightning that comes from the East . . .*", it appears, the water of the river Euphrates is dried up to prepare for the coming of the heavenly Kings – Father, Son and Holy Spirit, in other words, this is a description of the Second Advent.

We have already learned, that in Bible prophecy water is symbolic of many people or nations (see Revelation 17:15). Therefore, the drying up of this great river points to the drying up of the support of nations. As we will see in Revelation 17, the many nations that have given their help, aid and assistance to the false religions of the world will withdraw their support, because of the suffering caused by the plagues. The apostate religious leaders have been unable to prevent, or even affect, the plagues falling on themselves, and their followers, and now their own people turn on them. (More of this in Revelation 17.)

Revelation 16:13-16 – At this point, under the sixth plague, John sees a striking phenomenon. Three impure spirits, that look like frogs, come out of the mouths of the dragon, beast and false prophet. We have seen these three evil characters before in Revelation 13. They are none other than the fake Godhead – the devil, the Papacy and the false Protestant church.

John sees the demonic spirits, that come out of their mouths, performing miracles to deceive the kings of the world in order to gather them to a last battle against God's people. Once again, here is symbolic language describing literal actions and events.

Now the popularity of the three protagonists is waning, they form an unholy confederacy and make a last ditch attempt to rally the troops. What are the frog-like evil spirits that they spew from their mouths? As they come out of the mouths of the three characters, they could be spoken words. What we definitely know is they are demonic, and will perform miracles that will deceive the kings of the earth. Just as the magicians in Egypt, were able to use secret arts (or collusion with evil spirits) to replicate the first two plagues that God brought on the Egyptians, thereby causing Pharaoh to defy God (see Exodus 7:20-22 and Exodus 8:6,7), so the devil, beast and false prophet will use evil spirits to deceive the world's rulers at the end of time. Their deceiving wonders will succeed, for the kings of the earth will indeed gather for battle at a place called Armageddon.

There is widespread misunderstanding about the battle of Armageddon, usually thought of as the last global war that will destroy the planet, or perhaps a nuclear war between nations that leads to annihilation. However, Revelation 16:16 tells us that the Unholy Trinity lead the kings of the world (no doubt with their armies) to gather at a place called Armageddon, in preparation for the battle on the great day of God Almighty. The first point to realise here is, this is a religious war, not a war of nations. The devil, beast and false prophet are enemies of God's true church. They have sought to obliterate it throughout history. Now the Seven Last Plagues are falling on everyone, except God's people, and the Unholy Trinity are losing the support of the general populace. In desperation, they pull out all the stops and deceive the kings into joining with them to destroy the righteous people, once and for all.

Let us look at the word 'Armageddon'. It is a Hebrew word, also translated as Megiddo ten times in the Old Testament. The city of Megiddo was situated in the territory of Issachar near the river Euphrates. In the plains of Megiddo, many battles were fought between the Children of Israel and the surrounding idol worshiping nations. Therefore, symbolically Armageddon is an apt place for the setting of the final battle between God's people and the forces of evil.

The interesting thing about this battle is, it never actually takes place, for God intervenes. The 144,000 are no match for the combined forces of all the kings of the earth. Although the kings, and their armies, gather in readiness to decimate the people of God, they do not realise the date set for the battle is *"the great day of God Almighty"* (Revelation16:14), in other words, the day of the Second Advent. While the devil, beast and false prophet conspire with the political world rulers to bring about the genocide of God's people, they are unaware their plans will be interrupted by Jesus Himself. Revelation 16:15 are the words of Jesus. He warns:

"Look, I come like a thief!
Blessed is the one who stays awake and remains clothed,
so as not to go naked and be shamefully exposed."

The kings of the earth are spiritually naked and about to suffer public humiliation. Preoccupied with their own murderous intent, they totally miss the fact that Jesus is about to return to earth to rescue His people.

Revelation 16:17-21 – The Seventh Plague is poured into the air signifying that this plague affects the whole world. The voice of God is heard from the heavenly temple as it pronounces, *"It is done!"* Then come flashes of lightning, rumblings, peals of thunder, and a severe earthquake, which surpasses every earthquake that has gone before. These signs should now be familiar. We have seen them in the Sixth Seal (see Revelation 6:14-17) and the Seventh Trumpet (see Revelation 11:19), they herald the coming of Jesus. He rescues His people from the hands of the world's armies.

We are told that the effect of the tremendous earthquake splits the great city into three parts. Revelation 17:18 explains that the great city is actually Babylon the Great; the fallen woman of the Second Angel's Message (see Revelation 14:8). She is symbolic of false religion through the ages. At the time of the end, Babylon is composed of the Unholy Trinity – the devil, the

Roman Catholic Church and False Protestantism. They have been working in unison, but now the coming of Jesus breaks their union. They become three separate, powerless entities. Furthermore, Babylon the Great, the one who made the nations drink the maddening wine of false doctrine, is now given the cup filled with the wine of the fury of God's wrath. Poetic justice indeed.

At Jesus' coming all cities and nations collapse, every island and mountain is moved out of place. Huge hailstones, each weighing around 100 pounds, fall from the sky unto the people below, and the people curse God because of the hail, and because this plague is so terrible.

There are no words to express just how devastating the Seven Last Plagues will be; the destruction and appalling suffering they will cause. As Revelation 16:15 promises: *"....Blessed is the one who stays awake and remains clothed, so as not to go naked and be shamefully exposed."* Those who remain clothed wear Jesus' robe of righteousness. They will be eagerly awaiting the Second Coming, and so will not be taken unawares.

Now that you have read this chapter, there is no need for you to suffer the Seven Last Plagues. Now that you have received the warning, you need not be caught unawares and shamefully exposed. The plagues will fall on those who refuse to accept Jesus as their Saviour. Surely, the plagues are recorded in Revelation so that we can choose to be in the triumphant group standing before the throne of God, singing the song of deliverance and salvation.

Footnote:

Here are the ten plagues of Egypt and the Seven Last Plagues compared:

Ten Plagues of Egypt	Seven Last Plagues
First Plague: The river Nile, streams, canals, ponds and reservoirs turned to blood. All fish die.	**Second Plague:** The sea turns to blood and everything in it dies. **Third Plague:** Rivers and springs turn to blood.
Second Plague: Frogs swarmed the land.	Not included
Third Plague: Gnats on people and animals.	Not included
Fourth Plague: Swarm of flies.	Not included
Fifth Plague: All livestock died of plague.	Not included
Sixth Plague: Festering boils on people and animals.	**First Plague:** Ugly festering sores on those with the mark of the beast.
Seventh Plague: Hailstorm with thunder and lightning that killed people, animals, and all vegetation.	**Seventh Plague:** Huge hailstones fall on people; lightning and thunder.
Eighth Plague: Swarm of locusts that devoured all vegetation.	Not included
Ninth Plague: Darkness that could be felt covered the land for three days, so that people could not see each other.	**Fifth Plague:** The throne of the Beast covered in darkness so that people gnaw their tongues in agony.

Ten Plagues of Egypt	Seven Last Plagues
Tenth Plague: All first-born sons and animals died.	Not included
Not included	**Fourth Plague:** The sun allowed to scorch humanity.
Not included	**Sixth Plague:** The great river Euphrates is dried up to prepare the way for the Kings of the East. Three frog-like evil spirits come out of the mouths of the Unholy Trinity, that perform miracles in order to gather the world's kings to battle against God's people at Armageddon.
Not included	**Seventh Plague:** Signs of Jesus' coming: Tremendous earthquake that splits the evil confederacy; Babylon the Great is given the wine of God's fury to drink; every island and mountain moved out of place; cities and nations collapse.

Revelation Chapter Seventeen

THE PROSTITUTE AND THE SCARLET BEAST

Based on Revelation 17:1-18

Revelation 17 is the first in a trilogy of chapters dealing specifically with Babylon the Great.

In this chapter, we will examine the great prostitute, Babylon, and her accomplice, the scarlet beast.

The first time we met the prostitute was in Revelation 14:8, where we learned she is a fallen woman called Babylon the Great. As we know, women in Bible prophecy symbolise churches (see Ephesians 5:23-27), but unlike the pure woman in Revelation 12, who is the true church of God through the ages, the fallen Babylon represents the fallen, or apostate, church through time, that deceives people with its false and confusing doctrines.

Now it is clear who Babylon is, we can look closely, with John, at the rise and fall of this astonishing power.

Revelation 17:1 – An angel who held one of the bowls containing the Seven Last Plagues, tells John he is about to show him the punishment of the great prostitute who sits by *"many waters"*. 'Many waters' is another prophetic symbol we are familiar with. Revelation 17:15 tells us this symbolises a multitude of multi-national people. The prostitute, therefore, enjoys global popularity, but now the angel reveals Babylon is about to be punished.

Remember, we have reached the time of God's retribution. The time for mankind to repent has passed. God's people are now sealed in their decision to follow Jesus. Therefore, they are saved, and God can now unleash punishment on the unsaved of the earth.

Revelation 17:2 – The angel (who is probably the seventh angel from Revelation 16, as his plague brought about the punishment of Babylon) goes on to tell John that the kings of the earth committed adultery with the prostitute, and the earth's inhabitants are intoxicated with the wine of her adulteries. As Babylon represents a religious institution, the angel must be referring to spiritual adultery, which is, forsaking Jesus (the Husband of His church) to join with false gods and doctrines. Here we see the kings of the earth, or political rulers, entertaining false religions. Their actions are being heavily influenced by churches that teach error. The result is, global apostasy being championed by governments. No wonder the general populace is drunk with false religion.

Revelation 17:3 - The angel carries John away in vision. He is shown the prostitute, Babylon. She is in a wilderness, sitting on a scarlet beast. The beast reminds us of the first (or leopard-like) beast of Revelation 13, for it too is covered with blasphemous names and has seven heads and ten horns. And, of course, the seven heads and ten horns connect the scarlet beast to the person controlling the leopard-like beast – the devil. In Revelation 12, we saw him depicted as the enormous red dragon with seven heads and ten horns. Also, the fact that both the scarlet beast and the enormous red dragon are the same colour is further confirmation of where this beast's loyalties lie.

No doubt, all three beasts are working in harmony. The leopard-like beast we identified as the world ruling nations, which through history have reigned in opposition to God and His church, culminating in the reign of the Papacy (the second person of the Unholy/Counterfeit Trinity).

Revelation 17:4 – The prostitute is described. She is dressed in purple and scarlet, and is glittering with gold, precious stones and pearls. She holds a golden cup in her hand filled with abominable things, and the filth of her adulteries. It is clear the prostitute is wealthy, indicating the financial position of the false churches she represents. The golden cup, she holds, is alluring, but it holds teachings that are nasty and detestable to God. These are the doctrines that deceive the people of the world; stupefying and blurring their spiritual perception.

Revelation 17:5 – Just in case we are still unsure as to who this prostitute is, her name is revealed. Written on her forehead is her name, described by John as a mystery:

"Babylon the Great
The mother of prostitutes
and of the abominations of the earth."

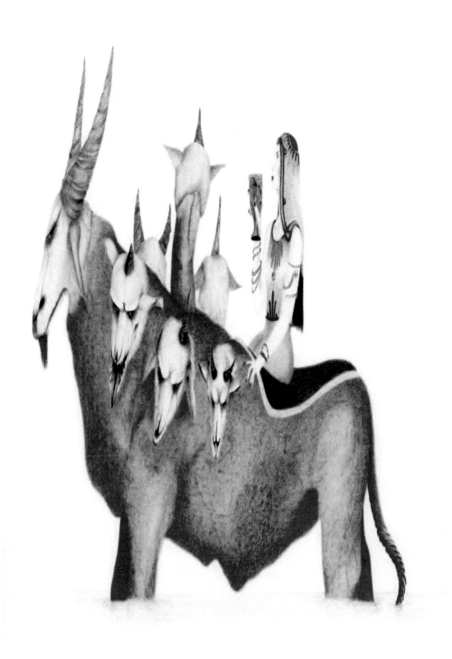

Yes, this is Babylon, called *"Great"* because of the magnitude of evil she has perpetuated throughout history. She is described as a prostitute for, as the apostate church, she has committed spiritual adultery by leaving the truth of Jesus and consorting with false doctrine. In this activity, she has partnered kings and governments, and grown rich in the process. Babylon, the false church, has spawned other apostate churches (including false Protestantism). Moreover, her children continue her work of deceiving the nations. As we have already seen, the apostate church, in the guise of Papal Rome, massacred the followers of God who opposed Catholicism during the 1,260 years of the Dark Ages: surely an abomination in God's eyes.

Revelation 17:6 – confirms the atrocities committed by the false church, for John sees Babylon drunk on the blood of God's holy people and those who bear testimony to Jesus. John is astonished at the actions of Babylon. As yet, he is unaware of the identity of this symbol.

Revelation 17:7 – The angel reassures John. He is about to reveal the mystery of both Babylon, and the scarlet beast she rides.

Revelation 17:8 – The angel begins with the scarlet beast who is described as *"once was, now is not, and yet will come up out of the Abyss, and go to its destruction. The inhabitants of the earth whose names have not been written in the Book of Life from the creation of the world will be astonished when they see the beast, because it once was, now is not and yet will come."*

There are differing views among Bible scholars regarding the meaning of the *phrase "once was, now is not and yet will come"*, but most agree this points to Rome. Similar language is used in Revelation 13:3 when describing the seventh head of the leopard-like beast that received a deadly wound which nevertheless was healed. This beast's head could also be described as *"once was, now is not and yet will come"*. When the seventh head of the leopard-like beast is resurrected, the whole beast revives and becomes the Roman Catholic Church of the end time. And, like the scarlet beast of Revelation 17, the whole world wonders after it because it comes to life after apparently being dead.

Revelation 17:9-10 – The angel gives further information on the scarlet beast. Remember, like the leopard-like beast, it has seven heads and ten horns. We identified its seven heads as the prominent empires opposed to God through history – Egypt, Assyria, Babylon, Medo-Persia, Greece, Pagan Rome, Papal Rome.

The angel first warns John that to understand what he is about to reveal, will take wisdom. In other words, it requires deep study and may be difficult to comprehend.

He says, the scarlet beast's seven heads are seven hills on which the prostitute sits. Rome is built on seven hills. However, the angel goes on to say, the seven heads are also seven kings; five of which are fallen, one is, and the other has not yet come, but when he does come, he will remain for only a little while.

If we continue with the above explanation of the seven prominent empires through time, then the five fallen kings would be Egypt, Assyria, Babylon, Medo-Persia and Greece, which indeed have fallen from global prominence. This would identify Pagan Rome, the world ruling empire during John's time, as the king that 'is', and Papal Rome the *"other"* that *"has not yet come"*. History bears out that Papal Rome succeeded Pagan Rome, which of course was a future event as far as John was concerned, and which he would not live to see. The fact that the seventh king would remain *"for only a little while"* could point to Pope Pius VI whose reign as Pope was cut short when he was taken into captivity in 1798.

Revelation 17:11 – The angel identifies the scarlet beast itself as the eighth king, who belongs with the seven heads/kings, and who is going to his destruction. The beast, then, appears to be the Roman power in its revived state. It is specifically, Rome during the end time; for it is the one that goes into destruction. As Papal Rome at the end of time will be included in Babylon as a false religious power, we can identify the scarlet beast specifically as political Rome. Therefore, Babylon's riding of the beast would signify the confederacy of false religion with the political power of Rome, working in unison against God's people just before Jesus returns. As false religion is riding the political power, once again, we are being shown the merging of State and religion in a quest for global dominance. Notice, that religion is the driving force behind political decisions and actions.

Revelation 17:12-13 – The angel then gives the explanation of the scarlet beast's ten horns. He says, they are ten kings who have not yet received their kingdoms, but will receive authority as kings along with the beast for one hour. They will give their power and authority to the beast because, like the beast, their aim is to destroy God's people.

If we are comparing the scarlet beast with the leopard-like beast of Revelation 13, which also has ten horns, we can conclude that the ten horns are the ten countries of Europe into which the Roman empire was divided at its demise (see Daniel 7:24). In John's day, these European nations had not yet come to power.

It is clear the nations of Europe will form an end time political alliance with Rome against God's people. There is some discussion as to whether the *"hour"* of their period of power is prophetic time (equivalent to 15 literal days) or just an indication of a brief period. Whichever interpretation is used, we can agree, this confederacy does not last long.

Revelation 17:14 – The angel unmasks the real aim of the evil confederation: it will wage war against the Lamb (Jesus), but the Lamb will triumph over it because He is Lord of lords and King of kings – *"and with Him will be His called, chosen and faithful followers."* This is another indication that although the false church, united with the political powers, will seek to attack God's people, it is Jesus who will triumph over them when He returns to earth.

Revelation 17:15 – We have used this text on a number of occasions to decipher a Bible symbol. The angel confirms the waters by which the prostitute sits are *"peoples, multitudes, nations and languages"*. Therefore, although John was figuratively taken to a barren wilderness to see the prostitute and the scarlet beast, as she is sitting beside many waters, clearly, the apostate church achieves global popularity. Perhaps then, the wilderness is symbolic of the barren state of the religion of this fallen church. It is devoid of the water of life, available only from Jesus (see John 4:13,14 and John 7:37).

Revelation 17:16-17 – Here is confirmation. Babylon will enjoy worldwide acclaim, but at the end, as we have already seen, during the sixth last plague, even her confederates will turn against her. Ultimately, both the scarlet beast and the ten kings will attack her. *"They will bring her to ruin and leave her naked, they will eat her flesh and burn her with fire."*

Revelation 17:17 – It is God who puts it into the hearts of Babylon's allies to tear down the apostate religious leaders. They will be accomplishing His retribution, as already shown in the seventh last plague (see Revelation 16:19).

Revelation 17:18 – The link between the destruction of Babylon and the destruction of the great city in the seventh last plague is reiterated, for the angel says, *"The woman you saw [Babylon] is the great city that rules over the kings of the earth."*

Bible scholars may not all agree on the interpretation of the various details of the scarlet beast, but the overall understanding of Revelation 17 is clear:

The apostate church, that has sought, through the ages, to obliterate truth, and all who follow it, will, in the end time, unite with governments in an evil union of church and State. The aim of this union is to finally annihilate God's people. This alliance will last only a brief time, and will be brought to an end when the political leaders, together with the nations they rule, turn on the false religious leaders to destroy them. In this way, they will fulfil the wrath of God promised in defence of His people.

Footnote:

IDENTIFICATION OF THE SCARLET BEAST

Bible Text	Description of the scarlet beast	Meaning
Revelation 17:3	The beast is scarlet	It is the same colour as the great red dragon (the devil) – Revelation 12:3,9. Therefore they are connected.
Revelation 17:3	The beast is covered with blasphemous names	It opposes God just like the leopard-like beast (the Papacy) – Revelation 13:1
Revelation 17:3	The beast has seven heads and ten horns	This is the same as the leopard-like beast and the great red dragon. Therefore they are connected (Revelation 12:3 and 13:1)
Revelation 17:8	The beast once was, now is not, and yet will come up out of the Abyss (the desolate earth Genesis 1:2, Jeremiah 4:24-27), and go to its destruction	Similar to one of the heads of the leopard-like beast that was alive, received a deadly wound and the wound was healed (Revelation 13:3). The scarlet beast will go to its destruction – this points to the final destruction in the lake of fire. Therefore it is a last day power
Revelation 17:8	The inhabitants of the earth (whose names are not written in the Book of Life) wonder at the beast because it once was, now is not, and yet will come	Similar to the leopard-like beast (Revelation 13:3)– the world wonders after the scarlet beast because it dies, but revives

Bible Text	Description of the scarlet beast	Meaning
Revelation 17:9	The beast's seven heads are seven hills on which Babylon sits	Rome is built on seven hills
Revelation 17:10	The beast's seven heads are also seven kings – five have fallen, one is, the other has not yet come, but when he does come, he must remain for only a little while	Like the leopard-like beast, the seven great nations who opposed God through the ages: Egypt, Assyria, Babylon, Medo-Persia, Greece, Pagan Rome, Papal Rome. In John's time, the first five had fallen from global prominence, and the sixth (Pagan Rome) was ruling. The seventh king (the Papacy) was not yet in power. The seventh who would remain for only a little while, could refer to Pope Pius V1 who was taken into exile
Revelation 17:11	The beast himself who once was, and now is not, is the eighth king who belongs to the seven and is going to his destruction.	The eighth king is Rome in its revived last day political form.
Revelation 17:12	The beast's ten horns are ten kings who have not received their authority yet.	The ten kingdoms of Europe who ruled after Pagan Rome. In John's time, they had not yet come to power.

Bible Text	Description of the scarlet beast	Meaning
Revelation 17:12,13	The ten kings will receive authority as kings along with the beast for only one hour.	The end time Western European kingdoms give over their authority to Political Rome because they have the same aim, but this confederacy will not last long.
Revelation 17:14	The ten kings and the beast will wage war against Jesus but they will be defeated by Him	The Western European kingdoms, and Political Rome, led by the Roman Catholic Church will seek to attack God's people, but Jesus will interrupt the planned attack with His second coming
Revelation 17:16	The beast and the ten kings will come to hate Babylon. They will attack her and bring her to ruin.	Political Rome and the European nations will finally turn on the false religious leaders during the sixth last plague (the drying up of the River Euphrates – Revelation 16:12)
Revelation 17:17	God has put it into the hearts of the ten kings to hand over their authority to the beast as this will culminate in their attack on Babylon	Because they are allied with Political Rome, the European kingdoms will follow it in hating the apostate church (Babylon), and carrying out God's retribution

Conclusion:

As Babylon is the apostate church through the ages, which includes the Roman Catholic Church in the end time, the scarlet beast must be Rome's political arm during the last days, that turns against the apostate church during the sixth last plague.

Revelation Chapter Eighteen

"COME OUT OF HER MY PEOPLE!"

Based on Revelation 18:1-24

We have arrived at the second chapter in the Revelation trilogy concerning Babylon the Great.

In Revelation 17, we saw the rise and fall of Babylon, and her connection with the scarlet beast. There is no doubt Babylon (false religion) is an evil power deserving our abhorrence, yet, there are devout and faithful people worshiping within Babylon. The complete gospel message has not yet been presented to them. They are therefore worshiping God in the only way they know. Many of these people do not understand that the Ten Commandments form the foundation of God's governance, and are as sacred as God Himself. Therefore, any attempt to change His law is an attack on the God they claim to worship. God is not willing to destroy these people before they have heard the entire gospel of salvation, and have the opportunity to join His true church.

Revelation 18 goes back to a time before the close of the Investigative Judgement, when the last gospel message is still being preached; in other words, to today. It is an amplification of the Second Angel's Message in Revelation 14:8.

Revelation 18:1-4 – John sees *"another"* angel coming down from heaven. He notes the angel has great authority and illuminates the earth with his splendour. 'Another' angel implies there were others before him. Moreover, as this angel's warning is a more detailed version of the Second Angel's Message (see Revelation 14:8), it is clear he belongs with the three angels giving the final gospel announcement. Once again, we must view this angel as symbolic of earthly messengers; for it is the responsibility of human beings to spread the good news of salvation (see Matthew 28:18-20, Acts 1:8).

It is significant this angel illuminates the world with his power: the effect of the dispatch he bears will enlighten the inhabitants of earth. The Three Angels' Messages have been preached since the Great Disappointment of 1844. However, Revelation 18 is set just before the fate of humanity is sealed, so now the three-fold gospel message must be preached with more force, more emphasis, and more power, because time is short; Jesus is soon to come.

Revelation 18:2-3 – This is the angel's message:

(i) *"Fallen! Fallen is Babylon the Great!"*

We are reminded that Babylon has fallen away from the truth. She fell when the church of God joined with Paganism during the time of Emperor Constantine, and fell again when the Protestant churches sought to rejoin the Catholic Church from which they separated. Babylon's fall progresses with time.

Revelation 12:17 (KJV) describes the true church of God as a small group (a remnant). In contrast, the apostate church is described as 'Great'. There are many false churches in existence, yet only one true church. Every church that deviates from Bible truth must, by definition, be a false church, and therefore included in Babylon. Also, Babylon is 'Great' in the evil it commits; it has ever been ready to persecute, oppress and kill its dissenters. It is 'Great' in the power it wields, and the wealth it owns.

Taking the Roman Catholic Church as our example, here is a quotation regarding the wealth of the Catholic Church in Australia from the 'Sidney Morning Herald' - 12 February 2018:

"The Catholic Church in Australia is worth tens of billions of dollars, making it one of the country's biggest non-government property owners, and massively wealthier than it has claimed in evidence to major inquiries into child sexual abuse. . . . The investigation was based on intricate data from local councils that allowed more than 1860 valuations of church-owned property in Victoria. That showed that across 36 municipalities - including nearly all of metropolitan Melbourne - the church had land and buildings worth almost $7 billion in 2016.

"Extrapolated nationally, using conservative assumptions, the church owns property worth more than $30 billion Australia-wide."

Babylon is 'Great' because of its popularity. Again, looking at the Catholic Church, it is reported its worldwide membership numbers 1.285 billion.

It is 'Great' because the leader of the world's largest church, the Pope, consorts with government leaders, heads of state and royalty, and advises them.

(ii) *"She has become a dwelling for demons*
**   *and a haunt for every impure spirit,***
**   *a haunt for every unclean bird,***
**   *a haunt for every unclean and detestable animal."***

It is a serious indictment for a church, purporting to worship God, to be described as a haunt for every unclean and hateful bird and animal. In Leviticus 11, God instructed His church regarding animals and birds fit for food, and therefore designated as clean. Yet, it appears the apostate church disobeys this instruction and welcomes the eating of every *"unclean"* meat. Reference to its being a *"dwelling for demons and ....every impure spirit"* denotes the false church's adoption of spiritualism within its ranks. The Bible tells us *"... the dead know nothing.....Their love, their hate and their jealousy have long since vanished; never again will they have a part in anything that happens under the sun."* (Ecclesiastes 9:5,6) Yet many churches support the un-Biblical

213

teaching of the immortal soul that continues to live on after death, and which can be contacted by the living. The Bible identifies this practice as *".....seducing spirits and doctrines of devils"* (1 Timothy 4:1 [KJV]).   As Babylon has fallen away from God and rejected Bible truth, only evil and spiritual impurity can dwell within it. The false church has lost all claims to holiness.

(iii) *"For all nations have drunk*
the maddening wine of her adulteries."

Every nation has become involved with false religion. Its deceiving doctrines cloud the spiritual understanding, benumb the senses and intoxicate the mind; much as wine makes one drunk.

(iv) *"The kings of the earth committed adultery with her"*

Babylon is an adulteress: she has strayed from God; taken up false doctrine; and is now joined in an unholy union with earth's political rulers.

(v) *"and the merchants of the earth grew rich from her excessive luxuries."*

The Catholic Church (a part of Babylon) is heavily involved in the business world. Here is a quotation from 'The Guardian Newspaper' – 21 January 2013:

"Few passing London tourists would ever guess that the premises of Bulgari, the upmarket jewellers in New Bond Street, had anything to do with the pope. Nor indeed the nearby headquarters of the wealthy investment bank Altium Capital, on the corner of St James's Square and Pall Mall.

"But these office blocks in one of London's most expensive districts are part of a surprising secret commercial property empire owned by the Vatican.

"Behind a disguised offshore company structure, the church's international portfolio has been built up over the years, using cash originally handed over

214

by Mussolini in return for papal recognition of the Italian fascist regime in 1929.

"Since then the international value of Mussolini's nest-egg has mounted until it now exceeds £500m. In 2006, at the height of the recent property bubble, the Vatican spent £15m of those funds to buy 30 St James's Square. Other UK properties are at 168 New Bond Street and in the city of Coventry. It also owns blocks of flats in Paris and Switzerland."

Revelation 18:4 – A call is made to God's people to come out of Babylon, so they will not share in her sins and receive the plagues soon to fall on the earth. God has people who are presently in false religions. We can compare this verse to John 10:16 where Jesus says:

"I have other sheep that are not of this sheep pen. I must bring them also. They too will listen to my voice, and there shall be one flock and one shepherd."

Clearly, God has faithful people scattered in other churches. Revelation 18 calls for them to leave Babylon and come to the true church. And, just in case anyone is confused about which church is the true church of God, Revelation 14:12 gives the answer. It is the church that
"....... keeps the commandments of God [all ten] *and remains faithful to Jesus".*

Revelation 18:5 – We are told the sins of Babylon are so great they are piled up to heaven, and God has now remembered her crimes.

Revelation 18:6 – Babylon will get back all she has given. She will be paid back double for what she has done. She will be poured a double portion from her own cup. For Babylon, it is certainly true that 'what goes around, comes around'. The false church has meted out death, destruction, war, persecution, torture and every kind of trauma possible. The promise is, it will receive all of this back in double measure.

Revelation 18:7 – God will give Babylon as much torment and grief as the glory and luxury she gave herself.
Here is what Babylon boasts in her heart:

"I sit enthroned as queen,
I am not a widow,
I will never mourn."

This suggests the false church believes it will always remain wealthy, independent, and never in need; it is oblivious to its imminent destruction.

Revelation 18:8 – warns that disaster will come upon Babylon swiftly and suddenly. This verse states that in *"one day"* the false church will receive her plagues, death, mourning and famine. She will be consumed by fire for God will judge her. 'One day' in this context appears to refer to the suddenness of the punishment Babylon will receive, rather than to the prophetic period of one literal year.

The warning confirms the demise of Babylon, already portrayed in Revelation 16, as she receives the seventh plague, and in Revelation 17 when her allies turn against her.

Nevertheless, there are those who will lament the demolition of Babylon. In the seventh last plague (see Revelation 16:19) Babylon is split into three parts as a result of her destruction. And, in Revelation 18:9-19 we see three groups involved with her who will mourn her passing.

Revelation 18:9-10 – The first group is *"the kings of the earth"* who committed adultery with her and shared in her luxury. They have been gaining wealth from consorting with the false church; getting rich from the business deals they engaged in together.

We are told they will *". . . see the smoke of her burning, they will weep and mourn over her. Terrified at her torment they will stand far off and cry:*

> *"Woe! Woe to you, great city*
> *you mighty city of Babylon!*
> *In one hour your doom has come!"*

Revelation 18:11-17 – The second group to mourn Babylon is *"the merchants of the earth"*. They have partnered the false church in trade and commerce in precious metals and gem stones, fine material, ivory, wood, spices, ointments, food, livestock, carriages, and even in human beings sold as slaves. Certainly, the merchants of the world have prospered from this business alliance.

It is interesting that the slave trade is mentioned here. Historically, some so-called Christians have attempted to justify the transportation of black slaves from Africa to the Americas during the 17th to 19th centuries; claiming slavery is sanctioned by God. Revelation 18 reveals more; the church itself was involved in human trafficking - surely one of the sins for which Babylon will be punished.

The merchants will weep and mourn for Babylon's lost splendour, and for their lost wealth, and cry out:

> *"Woe! Woe to you, great city,*
> *dressed in fine linen, purple and scarlet,*
> *and glittering with gold, precious stones and pearls!*
> *In one hour such great wealth has been brought to ruin!"*

Revelation 18:17-19 – The third group to mourn is the *"sea captains, and all who travel by ship, sailors, and all who earn their living from the sea"*. They will weep and mourn and throw dust on their heads for the loss of business, travel and employment Babylon afforded them. They will cry:

"Woe! Woe to you, great city,
where all who had ships on the sea
became rich through her wealth!
In one hour she has been brought to ruin!"

Notice that each lamenting group states Babylon will be brought to ruin in *"one hour"*, whereas earlier in the chapter (verse 8) we were told her plagues would overtake her in *"one day"*. As the 'one day' and 'one hour' describe the same event (the punishment of Babylon) this would seem to bear out the conclusion that these periods are not prophetic time but indications of the suddenness of the occurring destruction.

Revelation 18:20 – However, not everyone will lament the downfall of Babylon. Certainly, those in heaven will welcome the end of all the evil this false church has brought on the earth. To them, the fall of Babylon has long been awaited. And, there are others who have cause to rejoice over Babylon's demise, namely, the people of God, the apostles and prophets. They were denounced as heretics by the apostate church, and now God has judged her as the real heretic worthy of punishment.

Revelation 18:21-23 - John sees a mighty angel pick up a boulder, the size of a large millstone, and throw it into the sea. The angel then cries:

"With such violence
the great city of Babylon will be thrown down,
never to be found again.
The music of harpists and musicians, pipers and trumpeters,
will never be heard in you again.
No worker of any trade
will ever be found in you again.
The sound of a millstone
will never be heard in you again.
The light of a lamp
will never shine in you again.

The voice of bridegroom and bride
will never be heard in you again.
Your merchants were the world's important people.
By your magic spell all the nations were led astray."

The speech (or song) of the angel confirms the finality of the destruction of Babylon. The false church held such sway, wielded enormous power and influence, and was involved in every facet of life. It controlled so much of the lives of human beings, from the poorest to the greatest. Its passing will be a monumental event.

Revelation 18:24 – The last line of the angel's song is perhaps the most important reason for the punishment of Great Babylon:

"In her was found the blood of prophets and of
God's Holy people,
of all who have been slaughtered on the earth."

All those who are gaining from the wealth, trade, employment, leisure activities and enjoyment, created by the false church, should remember that it has led whole nations astray, and is therefore the cause of the eternal death of multitudes, and, it is responsible for the wholesale slaughter of God's holy people.

No wonder God warns anyone who is willing to listen to come out of her.

Revelation 18 gives a very clear picture of the demise of Babylon. False religion, personified as the prostitute riding on political Rome, is carefully described and shown to come to an abominable end (see Revelation 17). Those in God's church know this, and bear responsibility for proclaiming the angel's loud cry to those presently worshiping in churches where false doctrine is preached and practised. They have been appointed to let the truth be known, and call people out of the soon coming sudden destruction.

Revelation Chapter Nineteen

CELEBRATIONS AND DESTRUCTION

Based on Revelation 19:1-21

Revelation 19 is the last of three chapters dealing with the fate of Babylon, the apostate church. It is a chapter of celebration as heaven shouts 'Hallelujah!' for God's judgements. We will see other celebrations in this chapter, namely, a wedding, and a victorious battle procession.

Revelation 19:1-3 – After the destruction of the false church, Babylon, in the seventh plague, John hears a great roar from heaven. All the angels are shouting *"Hallelujah!"* (Praise the Lord). They cry:

> *"Salvation and glory and power belong to our God,*
> *for true and just are His judgements.*
> *He has condemned the great prostitute*
> *who corrupted the earth by her adulteries.*
> *He has avenged on her the blood of His servants."*

However, one celebratory shout is not enough; again they cry:

> *"Hallelujah!*
> *The smoke from her goes up for ever and ever."*

Once again, we see the finality of the destruction of false religion in the assurance that her smoke goes up for ever and ever. This tells us the false religious system will never return. It has corrupted the earth for too long. In Revelation 6:9,10, John saw the souls of the martyrs under the altar crying *"How long, Sovereign Lord . . . until you . . . avenge our blood?"* They were told to *". . . wait a little longer. . ."* In Revelation 19 all heaven acknowledges that God has kept His promise; the blood of His servants has been avenged.

Revelation 19:4 – The twenty-four elders and the four Cherubim, who, we know, are always around the throne of God, join in the celebration. They fall down before God in worship, and cry, *"Amen, Hallelujah!"*

Revelation 19:5 – John hears another voice coming from the throne, it cries:

"Praise our God,
all you His servants,
you who fear Him,
both great and small!"

As this call to worship refers to God in the third person, yet comes from God's throne, perhaps it is made by the angel Gabriel, the one who always stands in the presence of God (see Luke 1:19) covering His throne. We know angels cover the throne of God with their wings, because the Ark of the Covenant, made at God's instruction to house the Ten Commandments, had a cover called the Mercy Seat. On the Mercy Seat (the symbol of God's throne) were two sculpted angels, whose outstretched wings formed an arch over the Mercy Seat (see Exodus 25:10-22). The Ark of the Covenant was situated in the wilderness sanctuary, which, of course, is a pattern of the heavenly temple (see Hebrews 8:1-5). Therefore, we can conclude that in heaven, exalted angels stand next to God covering His throne (see Ezekiel 28:14 [KJV]).

This call for the servants of God (still living on earth) to join in the heavenly celebration (Revelation 19:5), includes us in the joyous thanksgiving. For we also should rejoice that the Great Babylon is no more. She has caused mayhem for thousands of years - we need fear her no longer.

Revelation 19:6-8 – Now that Babylon has been dealt with, heaven can announce the wedding of the Lamb. John hears a great multitude in heaven shouting. It sounds like the roar of rushing waters, and loud peals of thunder. The multitude shouts:

"Hallelujah!
For the Lord God Almighty reigns.
Let us rejoice and be glad
and give Him glory!
For the wedding of the Lamb has come,
and His bride has made herself ready.
Fine linen, bright and clean,
was given her to wear."

We are then told, *"Fine linen stands for the righteous acts of God's holy people."*

At this stage, the Investigative Judgement has been completed, and those who are saved have been decided in the judgement. Yet they remain on earth to go through the great persecution of the Time of Trouble, and witness the Seven Last Plagues. During the seventh plague, Great Babylon, the apostate church, has been totally destroyed. Now in heaven, before Jesus returns to earth, the celebration of the wedding of the Lamb takes place.

We have already noted that the Bible describes the true church as the wife of God or Jesus (see Isaiah 54:5, Jeremiah 3:14, 2 Corinthians 11:2). However, at this point, Revelation uses a new model; the marriage between the Lamb (Jesus) and the New Jerusalem, His bride (see Revelation 21:2,9). (We will examine the New Jerusalem in detail in Revelation 21.) What we now know is Jesus' bride is ready and adorned in fine, bright, clean linen which represents the righteous acts of God's people. It appears, this figurative wedding celebrates the readiness of God's people to join Him in heaven.

Revelation 19:9 – An angel instructs John to write the following as the true words of God. *"Blessed are those who are invited to the wedding supper of the Lamb!"* Although those saved from the earth do not attend the wedding itself, they are invited to attend the wedding supper. No doubt, this will take place when Jesus returns to earth to gather the faithful. He will lead them in a special procession to heaven where the wedding supper will take place. This follows the wedding ceremonies of ancient Israel, which consisted of two celebrations; the betrothal and the procession.

Revelation 19:10 – John, who is so overjoyed to witness the scene, falls at the feet of the angel in worship. But the angel quickly stops him and counsels him not to do it. The angel identifies himself as a fellow servant of God, just like John and all who follow Jesus. He counts himself as one of the brethren who hold to the testimony of Jesus. Only God is to be worshiped. It is certainly encouraging to learn that angels view themselves as equal with the saints of God. These superior beings identify with all those who have accepted Jesus as their Lord, they regard them as family.

The angel explains that it is the Spirit of prophecy who bears testimony to Jesus. All created beings, whether in heaven or on earth, have a duty to worship God, and hold on to the testimony of Jesus. This testimony is the truth as portrayed in the life of Jesus. The testimony is brought to us by the Holy Spirit through God's prophetic word. It follows, then, that the book of Revelation is included in the 'testimony of Jesus' (see Revelation 1:1,2).

From Revelation 19:11 to the end of the chapter, the vision skips forward to the third coming of Jesus to planet earth. (We will study the second and third comings in Revelation chapter twenty.)

Below is a chart of Jesus' purpose in visiting the earth three times:

First Coming	Second Coming	Third Coming
• To live as a human being, providing the example of how we should live. • To carry out His earthly ministry which included preaching the gospel and relieving human suffering. • To reveal the character of God to humanity. • To die for the sins of mankind, providing salvation for all and reconciliation with God. • To gain the victory over death by His resurrection. • To equip His followers to preach the gospel to the world.	• To raise from the dead all His people who have died (First Resurrection). • To take them, with the 144,000, to heaven. • The wicked who are alive will be struck dead.	• To bring His people back from heaven to live forever with Him on the earth made new. • To transport the New Jerusalem from heaven to earth. • To raise the wicked dead for sentencing (Second Resurrection). • To carry out sentence by burning the wicked (including Satan and his angels) in the Lake of Fire. • The Lake of Fire will eradicate sin from the earth. • The earth will be recreated.

We will now examine events and images describing the third coming of Jesus and the final destruction of the wicked.

Revelation 19:11 – Another scene appears before John. He sees heaven open up, and out rides a figure on a white horse (a sign of victory). The imposing rider is called *"Faithful and True"*. John is told the Rider judges and wages war using justice. This surely can only be Jesus.

Revelation 19:12-13 – tell us more about the Rider. His eyes are like blazing fire. This matches the description of Jesus in Revelation 1:14. The rider is wearing many crowns: we already know Jesus is the King of kings and Lord of lords. In addition, He has a name written on Him that no-one knows but He Himself. Jesus has many names; we know Him as Jehovah, Son of Man, the Lamb, the Messiah, the Good Shepherd, Immanuel, Son of God, to pick just a few, but here we are told Jesus has a secret name. No doubt the name is hugely significant, and perhaps refers to Jesus' success in carrying out the plan of salvation. He can now ride in triumph to carry out the plan's final stage. Whatever His secret name, Jesus keeps it to Himself.

Revelation 19:13 – Jesus is dressed in a robe dipped in blood. Well of course it is: Jesus spilled His blood to save humanity. We must always remember the price that was paid for us. And, here is final confirmation of who this figure is. His name is the *"Word of God"*. This name for Jesus is used in John chapter one: He is the Word of God, who is God Himself, our Creator and Redeemer.

Revelation 19:14 – Jesus is leading the armies of heaven. They also ride white horses, for through Jesus they have gained victory over sin. As proof of this, they are dressed in fine linen, white and clean. In verse 8 we were told this clothing stands for the righteous acts of God's holy people. The armies of heaven are none other than the redeemed from the earth. They were rescued from earth at Jesus' second coming. Now they triumphantly accompany Him at His third coming.

Revelation 19:15 – In His mouth Jesus holds a sharp sword with which to strike down the nations. This reminds us of Hebrews 4:12 *"For the word of God is alive and active. Sharper than any double-edged sword, it penetrates even to dividing soul and spirit, joints and marrow, it judges the thoughts and attitudes of the heart."*

Now we know why Jesus is using His name 'Word of God': He rides to earth, not only as a conquering King, but also as Judge. Moreover, His name shows how the wicked will be judged; by the truths written in the Bible.

In Exodus chapter twenty, the Children of Israel heard the voice of God speaking the Ten Commandments to them. His law is so important, He would not allow it to be proclaimed by Moses; He spoke it Himself and then wrote it on tables of stone, with His own finger (see Deuteronomy 9:10). When Jesus was on earth, He obeyed the law and taught us to do the same (see Matthew 5:17-19). His life fulfilled the written Word of God. Yet the Papacy sought to change God's law, and then at the end time, inspired the USA False Protestant church to force the world to follow the counterfeit Sabbath (Sunday), in direct opposition to the law of God. Now Jesus is coming to earth to let these false religious leaders know that the very law they tried to change, is the law that judges them.

Revelation 19:15 goes on to say, Jesus will rule the nations with an iron scepter. This refers to Psalms 2:9, which tells us God, will *"break the nations with a rod of iron; and dash them to pieces like pottery."* In other words, Jesus is coming to earth to finally destroy the wicked.

In Revelation 14, John saw the figurative destruction of the wicked as the harvesting of grapes thrown into a great winepress. Revelation 19:15 repeats this image. We are told Jesus treads the winepress of the fury of the wrath of God Almighty.

Revelation 19:16 – On Jesus' robe, covering His thigh, He has another name written; one we are familiar with:

"King of kings and Lord of lords"

This name declares, once and for all, who is Ruler of the earth. When the devil tempted Jesus in the wilderness, he claimed ownership of all the kingdoms of the world (see Matthew 4:8,9). Jesus rebuked him then, and, at His third

226

coming, the truth is displayed for all to see. Jesus is King and Lord of all the earth.

Revelation 19:17-18 – Give us another image of the final destruction of the wicked. John sees an angel standing in the sun, giving a loud command for the birds to gather for the great supper of God. They must eat the flesh of kings, generals, mighty horses and their riders, all people both free and slave, great and small. It is clear the people designated as wicked are found in every level of society. They are the ones who rejected offer after offer of salvation, and chose to be lost. Their end will be painful, and horrible to behold.

Revelation 19:19-20 – Among the wicked, John sees one of the main culprits, the beast (the Papacy), together with the kings of the earth and their armies. They are gathered together to wage war against Jesus and His saints. This is not the thwarted battle at Armageddon just before Jesus' second coming. It is another battle the devil tries to wage at Jesus' third coming, but we will learn more about this in Revelation 20.

Just as with Armageddon, the troops will gather, but the battle will not take place. Before one shot is fired, the beast and the False Prophet (the representatives of the False US Protestant church) are captured. We are reminded that the False Prophet is the one who brought fire down from heaven in order to deceive people into receiving the mark of the beast, and worshiping the False Protestant church. These two great deceivers, and persecutors of God's people, are together, thrown alive into the Lake of Fire described as burning with sulphur.

Revelation 19:21 – The kings of the earth, and their armies, are killed with the sword coming out of the mouth of Jesus, and all the birds gorge themselves on their flesh. Once again, figurative language is used here to describe the destruction of the wicked.

(As we will see in Revelation 20, all the wicked will be thrown into the Lake of Fire, from which there is no return.)

The imagery used in Revelation 19, as follows:

- judged or killed by the sword from the mouth of Jesus (the Word of God);
- ruled by an iron sceptre;
- crushed in the winepress;
- gorged by the birds of the air,

symbolise the final judgement, and the appalling nature of the deaths the wicked will suffer. The second death will be an extreme experience. None of us can imagine the terror it will evoke. Therefore, imagery we are familiar with, is used to help us comprehend just how horrifying it will be to die in this way.

The beast and False Prophet are singled out. Clearly, their time in the Lake of Fire will exceed the punishment of most.

The second death is graphically described for a reason. No human being need find themselves in the Lake of Fire; for it has been specifically prepared for the devil and his angels, not for mankind. Sin originated with the devil. He deceived one-third of the angels in heaven, who were thrown out of heaven with him. The Lake of Fire is reserved for them (see Matthew 25:41).

No-one will die in the fire by accident. Everyone there will have chosen their fate. Now that we understand the inevitable end of those who refuse to accept salvation, we can choose, right now, not to die in the Lake of Fire.

Revelation Chapter Twenty

THE MILLENNIUM

Based on Revelation 20:1-15

In this chapter, we will look at a very significant Bible time period of 1,000 years. In order for us to understand that we are referring to this particular period, we will call it 'The Millennium' (which of course means 1,000 years). The term 'The Millennium' is not used in the Bible.

Bible scholars hold varying views on The Millennium. This text will propose that, as the second coming of Jesus brings to an end the earthly system and the age of sin, there is no need to use prophetic time following the Second Advent. The 2,300 Days prophecy (see Daniel 8:14 and 9:24-27) foretells 22 October 1844 as the start of the Investigative Judgement, and also marks the end of Biblical time prophecies (see Chapter Ten). Therefore, this text promotes the view that The Millennium is a period of 1,000 literal years.

In Revelation 19, we saw the celebrations in heaven just before the Second Advent. Then we moved forward to the triumphal Third Advent. In Revelation 20 we will study the following:

- happenings on earth at Jesus' second coming;
- happenings in heaven during The Millennium;
- happenings on earth after The Millennium.

Revelation 20:1-3 – John witnesses a dramatic scene. An angel flies from heaven to earth holding a great chain. He seizes the devil, referred to by his various names (the dragon, that ancient serpent, the devil, Satan). We can be in no doubt of his identity.

The angel uses the chain to bind the devil for a thousand years (The Millennium). He throws the devil into the Abyss, and locks and seals it. Thus, the devil is prevented from deceiving the nations anymore until The Millennium ends.

At the end of The Millennium, the devil will be set free for a short time. What a scene!

231

Let us look at the word 'Abyss'. We have seen this before in Revelation 9, referring to a desolate place, and in Revelation 11, where the beast comes up from the Abyss, signifying a bottomless pit. Both references describe events on earth. We can therefore conclude that the binding of the devil will be on earth. There are instances in the Bible when the earth itself is described as an Abyss; in its formless stage before creation (see Genesis 1:1,2), and in the prophet Jeremiah's vision, when he sees the earth empty and desolate as a result of the Second Coming (see Jeremiah 4:24-27).

Revelation 6:12-17 also describes the ravaged earth at the Second Advent, when it once again becomes an Abyss.

Revelation 20:3 explains exactly how Satan will be bound; he will be kept from deceiving the nations for 1,000 years. As a result, the work he has engaged in, from the Garden of Eden until the Second Advent, will suddenly be brought to a halt. To understand how this will happen, we can look to other Bible texts which describe events at Jesus' coming.

1 Thessalonians 4:13-18 tell us, when Jesus comes, His feet will not touch the earth. First, the graves of the righteous dead will open, and those who have died as followers of Jesus, will be resurrected, and ascend to join Jesus in the air. Then the 144,000 (the righteous people still alive) will also be caught up to meet Jesus. Both groups will accompany Him to heaven.

2 Thessalonians 2:8 tells us that at the Second Advent, the wicked people who are living, will be instantly killed by the breath of Jesus' mouth, and the splendour of His coming. And, as we shall see later in Revelation 20, the wicked people already in their graves, stay there lifeless and unaware.

These Bible texts show that during The Millennium, the righteous will be in heaven with Jesus, and the wicked will all be dead. Therefore, the devil will have no-one to deceive; for there will be no people left alive on the earth. He will be bound to the earth, now a desolate Abyss, with nothing to do. We see, then, that the chain carried by the flying angel is a symbolic chain of circumstance; for the events of the Second Coming bring about circumstances that effectively bind the work of the devil.

For one thousand years, the devil (and his legions of angels) will be left to wander this dark planet, contemplating their fate. Nothing to do but bicker, and blame each other for their desperate and hopeless situation. No doubt, they will remember their evil deeds over the thousands of years of earth's history, and ponder just how long they will burn in the Lake of Fire for their despicable acts.

Revelation 20:3 goes on to say that once the thousand years have come to an end, the devil will be loosed for a short time. If the devil was bound because there were no living people to tempt, then at the close of The Millennium he can only be loosed if people come to life.

The event that brings the wicked back to life is the third coming of Jesus with His saints, which we saw in Revelation 19:11-14.

Revelation 20:4-5 – describe the work the righteous will be engaged in during The Millennium. John sees them sitting on thrones. They have been given authority to judge. They have gained this right because some were martyred for their faith (they came to life in the First Resurrection at Jesus' second coming), others refused to worship the Papacy and receive the mark of the beast. All have been faithful to Jesus, and now find themselves in heaven, judging the wicked during The Millennium.

Verse 5 also tells us the rest of the dead (that is the wicked dead people) did not come to life until the Second Resurrection at the end of the thousand years. This then confirms that at the end of The Millennium, when Jesus returns to earth with the saints (Jesus' third coming), the devil will be loosed, as all the wicked who have ever lived are resurrected to see Jesus come a third time. Remember, the wicked who were dead and buried before Jesus' second coming, stayed dead; they missed the Second Advent altogether, and so have not seen Jesus come in His glory. They now have the chance to see this wonder at His third coming.

Revelation 20:6 - John is told that those raised in the First Resurrection are blessed and holy. The second death (the Lake of Fire) has no power over them. They will be priests of God and of Christ, and will reign with God for The Millennium. As priests of God, they are like the Levites in ancient times, specially chosen to serve in the temple of God. Included in their reign will be the act of judging the wicked (see 1 Corinthians 6:2).

The judgement carried out by the righteous will not be to decide whether any of the wicked are eligible to be saved; God has already separated the righteous from the wicked before the Second Advent. During the Investigative Judgement (also known as the Pre-Advent Judgement because it takes place before Jesus' second coming) the books of those who profess to be followers of Jesus were examined to see if, (1) their profession was true, and, (2) they were indeed covered with Jesus' robe of righteousness, that is, they accepted Jesus' righteousness as their own. Those whose profession was found to be false, for they had not confessed all their sins, had their names removed from the Book of Life.

Those who made no profession of following Jesus were designated as 'wicked'. There was no need to examine their books in the Investigative Judgement, for they rejected Jesus. Deciding who will be saved (the saints), and who are the wicked, is God's work, and we can all be grateful this falls within His remit, as He is the only one able to judge justly. He knows our true motives and intentions. He knows those who belong to Him, and those who do not. He is the Righteous Judge.

However, during The Millennium, God graciously allows His saints to review the books of people's lives. The saints may have family members or friends whom they thought would be in heaven, but are not. The righteous will be able to look through the books and see every thought and action to verify that God has judged rightly. The books will also show the extent of wickedness of those left on earth. Justice must be seen to be done, therefore, God gives the saints access to the books so they can see for themselves. Later in Revelation 20 it is implied that included in the saints' work of judging, will be the responsibility of deciding the levels of punishment each wicked person will receive.

Revelation 20:7-8 – At the close of The Millennium Satan will be loosed from his prison – that is, at His third coming, Jesus will raise the wicked in the Second Resurrection. And immediately, the devil will go out to deceive the nations in the four corners of the earth. His army will comprise all the wicked who have ever lived; billions of people, described as the number of the sand on the seashore. The devil's aim is to gather them to battle against Jesus and the righteous saints with Him. This gathering to battle is termed *"Gog and Magog"*, and refers to Ezekiel chapters 38 and 39. Prince Gog, of the land of Magog, was an enemy of the Jewish nation who gathered a vast army from the surrounding nations, to fight against God's chosen people. In Ezekiel 38:9, Gog's army is described as *"advancing like a storm"* and *"like a cloud covering the land."* The Israelites did not have to fight the battle; God declared that He would intervene by bringing an earthquake, torrential rain, hailstones and burning sulphur on Gog and his troops.

Just as with Prince Gog, things will not go well for the devil and his army of lost souls. We could ask, why is the devil still fighting at this point? He must know he is already defeated, but it appears his thousand year holiday has given him time to hatch new plans. One can only imagine his persuasive arguments to the hoard of wicked people. Perhaps he tells them the odds are stacked in their favour, for they are in the majority. Their number may include the infamous generals from history, such as Genghis Khan, Napoleon, Hitler, Stalin, Pol Pot, Idi Amin, to name a few, who will believe the devil's lies, and decide their battle skills, and combined expertise, will lead to victory.

1 Corinthians 15:50-54 tell us that at the Second Coming all the righteous, who meet Jesus in the air, will receive perfect immortal bodies. Every mark of sin will be removed from their frames. Then, in heaven, mankind will once again have access to the Tree of Life (see Revelation 22:2). Thus, their fit, strong, healthy, beautiful bodies will be perpetuated throughout eternity. They will look very different from when they lived on earth. Meanwhile, the wicked, who remain unchanged, with their defects, illnesses, blemishes and deformities, will look a very sorry sight in comparison. When they compare themselves with the physical perfection of the righteous, this also may spur them on to attack God's people.

Despite all that has happened to Satan; his repeated defeats at the hand of Jesus, together with the certainty that he is headed for the Lake of Fire, he nevertheless remains unrepentant. He continues to fight against Jesus with every fibre of his being. His pride, selfishness and obstinacy will not allow him to yield.

Revelation 20:9 – Satan leads his army. They march across the breadth of the earth and surround the New Jerusalem, in which the saints are camped with Jesus. But, just as with Prince Gog, no battle takes place. Instead, fire comes down from heaven and devours them all.

Revelation 20:10 – The devil, who deceived the people into believing they could overthrow the city, is physically thrown into the fire, described as *"the lake of burning sulfur"*, joining the beast (the Papacy), and the False Prophet (the US False Protestant church). We are told they are tormented *"day and night for ever and ever"*. As already discussed in Revelation chapter fourteen, the Lake of Fire will not burn throughout eternity. Malachi 4:1-3 tell us the fire will burn itself out when the wicked people within its flames have died. Furthermore, Jude 7 says the cities of Sodom and Gomorrah were destroyed with *"eternal fire"*. And, as the fire that burned Sodom and Gomorrah, is not still burning today, but was quenched with the destruction of the cities, we must conclude that *"for ever and ever"* refers to the finality of the punishment. In other words, the effects of the punishment will last for ever and ever. Just as Sodom and Gomorrah were never rebuilt, so the wicked who die in the Lake of Fire will never be resurrected. This is the second death from which none of the unrighteous return. However, it appears the devil, the beast and the False Prophet (the Unholy Trinity) will spend a considerable amount of time in the fire before they are finally destroyed. Each wicked person will burn for an amount of time commensurate with the evil deeds they have committed (see Revelation 22:12). John sees the counterfeit Trinity burning day and night. It appears their punishment will last for days.

It is not pleasant to think about people burning in hell fire. However, God has warned that if we refuse to accept salvation, this will be our end. Therefore, the choice is ours. Sin must be eradicated, and unfortunately, those who insist on holding on to their sins will be burned up along with them.

Revelation 20:11 – The vision changes: we are taken back in time to a court scene. It is the executive judgement of the dead, which takes place on earth just before the fire falls from heaven. This is when specific punishment is meted out to those who have refused salvation.

John sees God seated on a great white throne. The earth and the heavens have fled from His presence. At Jesus' second coming the heavens were rolled up like a scroll and the mountains and islands moved out of place (see Revelation 6:14). It appears a similar disruption takes place at His third coming when God's great white throne is set in place.

Revelation 20:12 – John then sees the dead, both great and small, standing before the throne of God. The dead, of course, are the wicked who remained dead throughout The Millennium. They come to life in the Second Resurrection when Jesus returns to earth the third time. The books showing their deeds, which the saints examined in heaven during The Millennium, are now opened for the wicked to see. Then the Book of Life is opened, and they see for themselves, their names are not in the Book of Life.

Revelation 20:13 – John saw that the wicked were resurrected from both land and sea in order to face this judgement, and each was judged according to their deeds as recorded in their personal books.

Revelation 20:14 – Finally John watches 'Death' and 'The Grave' personified, thrown into the fire. Surely, this gives us reason to rejoice. No longer will humanity suffer death; no longer will we be destined to waste away in the grave. The redeemed are now immortal; they will live throughout eternity. John reminds us that the Lake of Fire is the second death in which even death itself is destroyed.

Revelation 20:15 – The final statement of the chapter is a solemn warning to us all. John says, anyone whose name is not found written in the Book of Life will be thrown into the Lake of Fire. As we now know, it is the people who have accepted Jesus as their Saviour who have their names recorded in the Book of Life.

The Millennium is a complex subject, not taught by many churches. It outlines the following:
- The First and Second Resurrections;
- The sentencing and execution of the wicked;
- The final end of the Unholy Trinity;
- The destruction of sin and death.

The detailed account of what will happen before, during and after The Millennium should make us determined to be included in the First Resurrection.

Those raised in the Second Resurrection will be destroyed along with the devil, his angels, and sin itself. Before they die, they will be given the opportunity to see for themselves why they should suffer eternal death. They will be reminded of the deeds that caused their names to be erased, or omitted, from the Book of Life. They will then acknowledge that God is a god of justice, and they have chosen their fate. Philippians 2:9-11 tell us, at that time, everyone in the universe who has ever lived, both the good, and the wicked (including the devil and his angels), will bow before Jesus and confess Him as Lord. Then the fire will descend.

Moreover, with the death of Satan, the creator of sin, and the obliteration of all the pain and misery he brought into the world, the planet can now be recreated; brought back to the beauty and perfection it had at the beginning of time.

Here is a chart of the events of The Millennium:

Before The Millennium	The Millennium	After The Millennium
Jesus' second coming. He comes to collect His saints and take them to heaven	The righteous are in heaven looking over the books of the wicked, and deciding their sentences	Jesus returns to earth with the saints (The Third Coming)
The righteous dead raised to meet Jesus in the air (The First Resurrection)	The wicked remain dead on earth	The New Jerusalem also descends to earth
Living saints caught up to meet Jesus in the air	Satan remains bound on earth; he has no-one to deceive	The wicked are raised to see Jesus' third coming (The Second Resurrection)
The righteous receive perfect, immortal bodies	The earth remains empty and desolate	The devil is loosed as now he has people to tempt
The wicked are slain by the splendour of Jesus' coming. The wicked dead remain in their graves	Earth at rest	The devil deceives the wicked to believe they can defeat Jesus and the righteous. The wicked surround the New Jerusalem
Satan is bound to the desolate earth by a chain of circumstance	The righteous have access to the Tree of Life	The wicked are sentenced in the executive judgement. All acknowledge Jesus as Lord. Fire falls from heaven on the wicked. Satan, his angels, the beast, and False Prophet are thrown into the Lake of Fire. All are destroyed
Earth is empty and desolate (The Abyss)	The saints live and reign with Christ in heaven	The fire cleanses the earth

Revelation Chapter Twenty-One

THE NEW JERUSALEM

Based on Revelation 21:1-27

Now that sin, sinners, and the originator of sin, have been burned out of existence, and the same fire has purified the earth, God can start again.

Revelation 21 is the penultimate chapter of the Bible. It is part of a select group of four chapters that show the world without the devil and sin. They are the Bible's first two chapters, Genesis 1 and 2, which describe the creation of the earth in the beginning, and its last two chapters, Revelation 21 and 22, describing the earth made new after sin has been eradicated forever. These chapters envelope the rest of the Bible, which catalogues man's attempt to live in, and deal with, a sin filled world.

Now in Revelation 21, the struggle is over; we can relax. We need not fear, for there is nothing, and no-one, capable of harming us. God will now remake the earth: it will be as it was before sin entered the picture. In fact, it will be better, because God will live here with His people.

Revelation 21:1 – John sees a new heaven and a new earth. After the Lake of Fire has burned itself out, a beautiful new earth emerges. It is the earth recreated, and not only the earth, but its atmospheric heavens too. The man-made pollution progressively destroying the earth's ozone layer has necessitated the creation of a new atmosphere around the earth.

John remarks that the first heaven and earth have passed away. This is not a patched repair job: everything is brand new. And one detail John notices immediately is, there is no longer any sea. John was on the Isle of Patmos, a penal colony where the sea formed the walls of his prison. Now he can celebrate; the great seas are no more. Planet earth, presently referred to as the blue planet of our solar system, because of its massive oceans, will look very different when recreated.

Revelation 21:2 – Next, John sees the Holy City, the New Jerusalem, descending from heaven to the earth. We first saw the New Jerusalem in heaven in Revelation 19 - the bride at the wedding of the Lamb. This is now confirmed, as in Revelation 21, John describes the New Jerusalem as *"prepared as a bride beautifully dressed for her husband."* The figurative marriage between the Lamb (Jesus), and the Holy City, symbolises the union of Christ with His church. The marriage ceremony took place in heaven just before Jesus' second coming. Remember, God's righteous people were still on earth at the time, therefore, the New Jerusalem took their place in heaven as Christ's bride. She is a fitting symbol, for she is not the old earthly Jerusalem, tainted with the sinful acts of men; she is created anew and adorned in material signifying the righteousness of the saints.

The descent of the New Jerusalem from heaven to earth must take place at Jesus' third coming following the Millennium, for the wicked who come to life in the Second Resurrection, surround the Holy City in their effort to destroy Jesus and His people (see Revelation 20:7-9). Also, as we know that Jesus is accompanied by the saints at His third coming (see Revelation 19:14), we can confidently state that at the Third Advent Jesus descends to earth with the righteous, and the New Jerusalem also descends at the same time. Just in case you were wondering where the Holy City will land, Zechariah 14:4 tells us Jesus will descend to the Mount of Olives (east of the present site of Jerusalem). When His feet touch the mount, it will split in two from east to west forming a great valley. The New Jerusalem will rest in the newly formed valley. Then Zechariah 14:5 confirms *". . . the Lord my God will come, and all the holy ones with Him."*

Revelation 21:3 – John, once again, hears the loud voice from the throne (possibly the voice of the Covering Angel, Gabriel). He says:

"Look!
God's dwelling place is now among the people,
and He will dwell with them.
They will be His people, and God Himself will be with them and be their God."

God is moving house. No longer will He be in a separate place, called heaven. Heaven (the place where God dwells) will now be situated on earth. How wonderful for the saints. By faith, they believed in God's existence, but their sinful state prevented them being in His presence. Now that sin no longer exists, there is no barrier to separate God from His people. He will dwell with humankind.

Revelation 21:4 – God will wipe away every tear from the eyes of the saints. There will be no reason to cry, for there will be no death, no mourning, no pain, no misery: the old order of things has passed away. This will truly be a new life. It is difficult to imagine what this new world will be like. We are so used to living in a world where evil abounds with its injustice, violence, unfairness, poverty, pestilence, war, dishonesty, abuse, discrimination, prejudice, and much, much more.

Revelation 21:5 – John is directly addressed by God who instructs him to write down the following words because they are trustworthy and true:

"I am making everything new!"

God reminds John he is to record what he sees and hears because it is all true. We also need to be reminded that a time is coming, soon, when there will be no more sin, God will dwell with us, and nothing bad will ever happen again. This is no fairy tale: it will happen.

Revelation 21:6-8 – God then confirms who He is, His gift of salvation, and the consequences of accepting the gift, or rejecting it. Surely, this is part of the trustworthy and true message John was reminded to write, for it is a crucial message for humanity today.

Even as God gives details of the new earth, He takes time to plead with us to accept salvation. He says:

"It is done.
I am the Alpha and the Omega,
the Beginning and the End.
To the thirsty I will give water without cost
from the spring of the water of life.
Those who are victorious will inherit all this,
and I will be their God and they will be My children.
But the cowardly, the unbelieving, the vile,
the murderers, the sexually immoral,
those who practice magic arts, the idolaters
and all liars – they will be consigned
to the fiery lake of burning sulfur.
This is the second death."

How could it be said that God is uncaring? He constantly calls us to accept Him in our lives. It is the only way we will be saved from eternal death, and He is reluctant to give us up. Clearly, God loves us. He wants us to live.

Revelation 21:9 – John is approached by one of the angels who carry the bowls with the Seven Last Plagues. He offers to give John a guided tour of the Holy City.

Revelation 21:10 – John follows the angel, and in vision, is taken to a high mountain. There he views the New Jerusalem coming down out of heaven.

Revelation 21:11-14 - Here is John's description of the city:

- It shines with the glory of God, which has the appearance of a precious crystal clear, jasper, jewel stone;
- It is surrounded by a great, high wall with twelve gates; three on the north, three on the south, three on the east, and three on the west;
- At each gate an angel is positioned;

- The twelve gates are named after the twelve tribes of Israel;
- The city has twelve foundations, each one named after a disciple of Jesus.

As John views the New Jerusalem coming down, he is able to take a close look at its foundations before they settle into the earth.

Every feature of the Holy City denotes its connection with the people of God through the ages. Ancient Israel was divided into twelve tribes. Moreover, in New Testament times Jesus chose twelve disciples to carry the gospel to the world. All are remembered in the city of God, and link the city with the depiction of God's true church in Revelation 12. The New Jerusalem, which in heaven represented the church, is now brought to earth, where God will live with His people.

Revelation 21:15-21 – The angel, showing John the vision, suddenly produces a measuring rod. He is going to measure the city for John. We have seen this type of measuring before. In Revelation 11:1 John was instructed to measure the heavenly temple. This happens when God seeks to confirm the reality of the object we are viewing. In this case, the measuring rod is made of gold. The New Jerusalem, built from precious metals and jewels, deserves a golden measuring rod:

- The city is built in a perfect square; each side measures 1,400 miles;
- Its city walls are 1,400 miles high, and 200 feet thick;
- The walls are made of jasper;
- The city itself is made of the purest (glass-like) gold;
- Each of the twelve foundations is decorated with a precious gem stone (jasper, sapphire, agate, emerald, onyx, ruby, chrysolite, beryl, topaz, turquoise, jacinth, amethyst);
- Each of the twelve gates is made of a giant pearl.
- The main street going through the city is made of gold that resembles transparent glass.

What a sight this must have been for John; a golden city of mammoth proportions, rides on jewelled foundations.

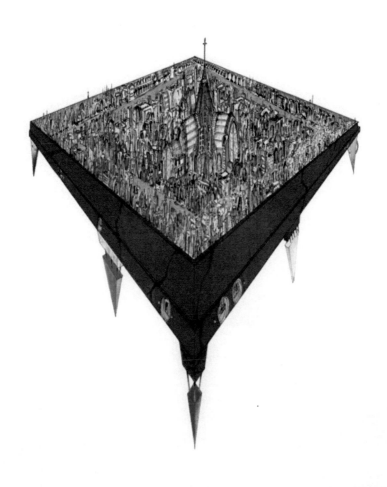

247

Revelation 21:22-26 – John looks for a temple within the Holy City. After all, the heavenly temple has played a major role in his visions. However, he cannot find it. He concludes the Lord God Almighty, and the Lamb, are its temple. We have been told over and over again that God will now dwell with His people throughout eternity. In ancient times, God instructed the Children of Israel to build a sanctuary so that He could dwell with them (see Exodus 25:8). Solomon built a magnificent permanent structure (mid-10th century BC), to enable the people to meet with their God. Then, when the Jews returned from captivity, they rebuilt the temple in around 515BC, so that once again they could be near their God.

Since the destruction of the Jewish temple in AD70, the gospel has spread around the world, and the real temple in heaven has been where God has met with His people; for their prayers have ascended to Jesus, our High Priest, as He intercedes for us before God (see Hebrews 7:24-25). Then, with the beginning of the Investigative Judgement in 1844, the focus has been on the Most Holy Place of the heavenly temple, where God judges His professed people (see Daniel 7:9-10,22).

However, in the earth made new, God physically dwells with His people, and communicates with them face-to-face. What need do we have of a temple? We can meet with the Godhead whenever we like. Gone are the ceremonies and types. No representation is required. We have the real deal - God will dwell among us.

- Because the city is alight with the glory of God and Jesus (the Lamb), it needs no sun nor moonlight;
- All nations of the earth, and their kings, will walk in the light of the city, and bring their own splendour to it;
- As there will be no night there, the gates will never be shut;
- The glory and honour of the nations will be brought into it.

Here we find references to Isaiah 60:10,11, where the prophet predicts the rebuilding of ancient Jerusalem will allow the nation to regain its former prestige. Isaiah states the great kings and nations will once again visit the city, bringing great wealth and glory to it. Its gates would remain open day and night to allow the numerous nations to continually bring their wealth. Therefore, Jerusalem would once again enjoy the renown it lost during the time of its captivity.

In comparison, the New Jerusalem will possess glory, honour and prestige beyond anything ever experienced, or even imagined. The righteous people of the world from all nations, whether they be former kings or commoners, will delight to share in the magnificence, grandeur and splendour emanating from the city.

Revelation 21:27 – The final verse of the chapter is a warning. John states, nothing impure will ever enter the Holy City. No-one who acts shamefully or deceitfully will be there. Only those whose names are written in the Lamb's Book of Life will be able to enter the New Jerusalem.

There is no getting away from it. God keeps telling us, if you want to be saved and be part of the wonderful scene of Revelation 21; give your life to Christ. Confess your sins to Him and ask that He cover you with His righteousness.

It's as simple as that.

Revelation Chapter Twenty-Two

"YES, I AM COMING SOON!"

Based on Revelation 22:1-21

We have arrived at the final chapter of Revelation, and also the conclusion of the entire Bible. How does one end an inspired book – the greatest book of all time? God has chosen to close His book with a happy ending, and a final promise.

In this chapter John's vision of the New Jerusalem continues, followed by the book's epilogue.

Revelation 22:1-2 – The angel shows John the interior of the New Jerusalem. The thrones of God the Father, and the Son, are situated within the Holy City. Issuing from their thrones is the river of the water of life, described as *"clear as crystal"*. The river flows down the middle of the main street of the city. We can refer here to the story of Jesus speaking with the woman at the well (see John 4:4-30). Jesus promised the woman that He was the originator of the living water that would quench her thirst forever. In other words, Jesus identified Himself as the means of salvation. Even in the New Jerusalem, we will ever be reminded that salvation comes only through Jesus; for the living water emerges from the thrones of God, and the Lamb.

Next, we see the Tree of Life; also in the New Jerusalem. It stands on each bank of the river. How can one tree stand on both sides of the river? Perhaps it is a tree with two trunks; each trunk planted on opposite banks, with its branches meeting together over the river, thus forming an archway.

Access to the Tree of Life confirms immortality for all the saved. The tree is referred to as 'the' Tree of Life: we must therefore assume it is the same tree formerly positioned in the Garden of Eden. Adam and Eve were barred from the tree after they sinned, and angels guarded it with a flaming sword to stop sinners gaining access to it (see Genesis 3:24). John sees the tree repositioned; it now stands in the New Jerusalem, where all God's people can eat of its fruit; for every one of them has been granted eternal life.

The Tree of Life bears twelve different crops of fruit; a new crop each month. We are told the leaves of the tree are for the healing of the nations. Ranko Stefanovic in the 'SDA Bible Study Guide 2019' on the Book of Revelation, gives a suggestion regarding the healing leaves of the Tree of Life:

"This healing does not refer to disease, as on the new earth there will be no disease. It refers to healing of the wounds caused by the barriers that have torn people apart throughout history. The redeemed of all ages and from all nations now belong to one family of God."

Let us picture the scene of the saints of God meeting around the Tree of Life, plucking its new monthly fruit. As they sit together under its leafy shade, they have time to learn of each other's national customs, cultures and practices. They will begin to understand, accept and value their differences. All that has historically separated the nations will now be the cement that binds them together as they see beauty in diversity – "*and the leaves of the Tree are for the healing of the nations.*" – What a wonderful scene.

Revelation 22:3-4 – The earth will no longer suffer the curse of sin. This curse was pronounced on Adam, Eve, and the earth, when they disobeyed God (see Genesis 3:9-19). With the obliteration of sin, the curse is lifted.

And, once again we are reminded that the throne of God, and of the Lamb (Jesus), will be in the city, and His servants will serve Him. God will be totally accessible to His people. They will be able to look on His face, and His name will be on their foreheads. We saw in Revelation 14:1 that the symbolic seal of God is the name of God and His Son written on the forehead, signifying that each one of His saints is in a personal relationship with God. They belong to Him and live in accordance with His principles. This relationship will continue throughout eternity.

Revelation 22:5 – We are reminded that within the city the source of light will be the Lord God, therefore we will not need the natural light of the sun, nor any artificial light.

The saints will reign for ever and ever.

This statement of victory concludes the final vision given to John.

The Epilogue of the Book of Revelation

We were told at the beginning of Revelation that Jesus would be revealed to us, and that this was a special revelation from God specifically for His church. The message came from God, was given through Jesus, and relayed to John by an angel. John was then caught up in the power of the Holy Spirit in order to view the visions.

(Just a note here, we will assume the angel, used for the relaying of the visions, is Gabriel, as he performed a similar function in revealing end time prophecy to Daniel [see Daniel 8:15,16]).

Now, at the close of the book, both the angel Gabriel and Jesus converse directly with John in order to complete the revelation. The practice of Gabriel being joined by Jesus to conclude a prophetic message appears to be heaven's method of confirmation and closure, as this was also done in the epilogue of the prophetic book of Daniel (see Daniel 12:5-13).

Revelation 22:6 – Gabriel confirms to John that all he has been shown is *"trustworthy and true"*. He states, the Lord God, who inspires the prophets, sent him to John to show the events of the future that will shortly begin to take place. And indeed, the letters to the seven churches, existing in Asia in John's time, began the messages of Revelation.

Revelation 22:7 – Jesus then interjects. He says:

> *"Look I am coming soon!*
> *Blessed is the one who keeps the words*
> *of the prophecy written in this scroll."*

Why would Jesus announce to John that His coming is *"soon"*? Nearly 2,000 years have passed since the book of Revelation was written. Was it therefore misleading to emphasise the nearness of His return? The point is, the Second

Advent must always be an urgent event. It is imperative each human being believes in the possibility of it happening within their lifetime, because once we have died, our salvation is decided. We have only the period of our lifetime to be saved, and as we have no idea how long that period will be, the coming of Jesus is 'soon' for us all. If we always keep in mind that Jesus' return is imminent we will remain in a state of readiness, and the words of the prophecies of Revelation will be a constant blessing to us.

Revelation 22:8-9 – John assures us he is the one to whom the messages have been entrusted. He eagerly confirms his eye witness status: he has both heard and seen the God-given visions. Now he is aware they have come to an end, he is awestruck, and again falls down to worship at the angel's feet. And once again, Gabriel stops him. He warns John not to do this, for he is a servant of God, just like John and his fellow prophets. Gabriel says "*Worship God!*"

Revelation 22:10 – As Gabriel declared his final words to Daniel at the close of his prophetic messages, Daniel was instructed to seal up the book until the time of the end (See Daniel 12:9). In other words, the prophecies given to Daniel were not meant for his time. As we saw in Revelation chapter ten, there came a time when the prophecies of Daniel were unsealed, for the time of the end had arrived.

In contrast, Gabriel tells John NOT to seal up the messages he has received, because the time of their fulfilment is near. The prophecies of Revelation stretch from John's time to the earth made new; they must be made available to all those seeking the truth of God.

Revelation 22:11 – Next, Gabriel gives the pronouncement that will be made once the Investigative Judgement is completed and the fate of each individual decided:

"Let the one who does wrong continue to do wrong;
let the vile person continue to be vile;
let the one who does right continue to do right;
and let the holy person continue to be holy."

The Investigative Judgement is going on in heaven right now. Therefore, we still have the opportunity to gain salvation and be covered with the blood of Jesus. Once the judgement is finished, each person's character will be fixed. They will remain as they are, never to change. Even at the close of the book, God is pleading with us to be saved.

Revelation 22:12 – Jesus adds His warning:

"Look I am coming soon!
My reward is with me,
and I will give to each person
according to what they have done."

When Jesus comes, the case of every human who has ever lived, will have been decided; for He brings each person's reward with Him. At the Second Advent no judgement will be made about who will accompany Him to heaven. He will come with the knowledge of who belong to Him, and who do not.

Revelation 22:13 – Jesus once again gives His credentials:

"I am the Alpha and the Omega,
the First and the Last,
the Beginning and the End."

Jesus identifies Himself as Almighty God; He is the self-existent one; He has always existed; He will always exist. We can trust what He says is true.

Revelation 22:14 - As part of His appeal to us, Jesus confirms exactly who will receive salvation:

"Blessed are those who wash their robes,
that they may have the right to the Tree of Life
and may go through the gates into the city."

Those who wash their robes are, of course, those who have given their characters to God. They have confessed their sins, and accepted the sacrifice of Jesus in their stead. They now wear the white robes of righteousness (see 1 John 1:9).

Revelation 22:15 – And here are those who will not be saved:

"Outside are the dogs,
those who practice magic arts,
the sexually immoral, the murderers,
the idolaters and everyone who loves
and practices falsehood."

Jesus could not make it more plain. Those who have chosen to keep their own character will be left outside the Holy City. Anyone reading these two descriptions will know in their heart of hearts which category they fall into.

Revelation 22:16 – Jesus again identifies Himself, and states why His testimony is credible:

"I, Jesus, have sent my angel to give you
this testimony for the churches.
I am the Root and the Offspring of David,
and the bright Morning Star."

He is the originator of the message. He has authorised His angel to give the visions to John, so that he can pass them on to His church through the ages. Jesus is the Son of God, and equal with God. He created king David, and as the Son of Man (the Lamb and Saviour of the world), He was born from the line of David. As the bright Morning Star, He is the Light of the World, the one who gives the light of truth to everyone in the world (see John 1:9-11).

257

Revelation 22:17 – Here is the final call and invitation to all mankind:

"The Spirit and the bride say, 'Come!'
and let the one who hears say 'Come!'
Let the one who is thirsty come;
and let the one who wishes
take the free gift of the water of life."

It is clear that all who read this book are given the opportunity to gain eternal life. The Holy Spirit is constantly speaking to each one inviting them to say 'yes'. The unequalled beauty of the New Jerusalem invites us to come inside and take up residence. Those who hear and accept the call have a duty to pass on the invitation to others. Those who have tasted all the world has to offer, and yet are still thirsty for something better, are invited to 'Come'. And, anyone who wants to, is invited to accept the free gift of salvation.

The call goes out to everyone.

Revelation 22:18-19 – And now comes the warning. The testimony of Revelation is God-given, and must not be tampered with. Those who seek to add their own teachings to the message, will receive the Seven Last Plagues. Equally, those who seek to take words out of the message, so that it is not read or heard in its entirety, will lose their right to enter the New Jerusalem, and eat of the Tree of Life.

Revelation 22:20-21 – Jesus' last words to the world are:

"Yes, I am coming soon!"

Surely, we must get the message. Time is running out for each one of us. We all must make a decision regarding where we intend to spend eternity. With all we have been shown, we can now make an informed decision.

John's decision is made. He says *"Amen. Come Lord Jesus."* This is the response of one who has decided they will spend eternity with Jesus. And, all who accept the salvation offered by God, will look forward to seeing Jesus come in the clouds of heaven.

The book of Revelation has been a message to God's church, and now John joins in addressing the saints. He pronounces a blessing on them:

"The grace of the Lord Jesus be with God's people. Amen."

The entire book of Revelation is a love letter from God to His church.

Following Jesus' ascension to heaven, He knew that without His physical presence through the ages to come, the church would need heavenly guidance to ensure its survival, until He returned to earth to rescue His faithful ones. Therefore, the messages of Revelation were given to John to encourage the church, lead God's people, and keep them true to Him despite the unfavourable, and even life threatening circumstances they would encounter.

The visions reveal the condition of God's church, and the external forces impacting it. They detail how the church will be attacked, persecuted and almost extinguished. The origins of its tormentors are exposed. We are told how the saints will be tempted and tortured at the end of time, the final great trial, and their victory through faith in Jesus and adherence to the law of God.

Finally, the book describes the reward reserved for the saints; as they inherit eternal life and dwell with the Godhead forever on the earth made new.

The visions of the book have been preserved, and protected from those seeking to destroy its truths. Its messages are revealed in symbols, and the keys to the explanation of each symbol are given to those who carefully, patiently and prayerfully search the scriptures.

The book of Revelation is a testimony from Jesus, showing deep affection and concern for His church.

Anyone reading and understanding this testimony can be in no doubt of God's love for humanity. Those who read and believe His word are those who will receive the grace of the Lord Jesus Christ.

Amen!

TABLE OF REVELATION'S PROPHETIC SYMBOLS

SYMBOL	MEANING	BIBLE REFERENCE
7 Golden Lampstands	The 7 churches of God	Revelation 1:20
7 Stars in the right hand of Jesus	The 7 angels (or leaders) of the 7 churches	Revelation 1:20
Time periods in prophecy	Day/Year principle (one prophetic day = one literal year)	Numbers 14:34, Ezekiel 4:6
A woman	A church	Ezekiel 16, Jeremiah 6:2, Ephesians 5:25-27
A virtuous woman	God's true church	Revelation 12:1
A prostitute	A false church	Revelation 17:3-6
Destructive winds	God's destructive judgements on the nations	Jeremiah 25:31-32
Trumpet blasts	A battle cry warning of great destruction	Jeremiah 4:19-21
Burning mountains (volcanoes)	Destroying nations	Jeremiah 51:25
Shooting Stars	Ungodly leaders	Jude 1:12,13
Flying Eagle ready to swoop	Pending disaster	Hosea 8:1, Habakkuk 1:8,9
The Abyss or Bottomless Pit	The earth in a desolate state	Genesis 1:2, Jeremiah 4:23-26
Smoke that causes darkness	Evil and Error	John 3:19, 1 Peter 2:9
Beasts	Earthly kingdoms	Daniel 7:17
Tails	Deceiving Prophets	Isaiah 9:14,15
Swarms of Locusts	Arabian Tribes	Judges 6:5,6, Judges 7:12
The enormous Red Dragon	The devil	Revelation 12:9

SYMBOL	MEANING	BIBLE REFERENCE
Multiple heads on beasts	Kings/Rulers/kingdoms	Revelation 17:10
Multiple horns on beasts	Kings/Rulers/kingdoms	Revelation 17:12
Crowns	Royalty	Revelation 19:12,16
Wings	Swift travel to flee danger. Safe keeping	Exodus 19:4, Deuteronomy 32:11
Water/Seas	Multitudes of people from different nations	Revelation 17:15
Earth/Wilderness (the opposite of water)	Sparsely populated region	Revelation 12:6

Index

Theme	Chapter(s)	Page Numbers
G		
God's true church	2, 3, 6, 12, 14, 16, 17, 18, 19, 21	17, 22-23, 25, 57, 148, 175, 179, 193, 198, 211-212, 225, 222, 245
God the Father	1, 3, 4, 5. 6. 7. 8, 13, 22	1-2, 6, 26-27, 31, 35-36, 39, 43, 45, 48-50, 52, 66, 70-71, 84, 155, 250
Great Controversy between God's Church and the devil, The	12	132-148
Great Disappointment, The	10, 14, 18	113-116, 171, 173, 179, 212
Great Red Dragon, The	12, 13, 17	132-148, 149, 153-154, 156, 159, 207,
H		
Heavenly Sanctuary/Temple, The	1, 3, 4, 5, 6, 7, 8, 9, 10, 11, 14, 15, 16, 19, 20, 21	10-11, 30-31, 38-39, 43, 48, 52, 79, 84, 99, 114-115, 128, 173, 181, 187-188, 194, 221, 234, 245, 248
Hell Fire	1, 6, 12, 14, 20	10, 57, 144, 177-180, 192, 237
Holy Place, The	1, 3, 4, 5, 8, 9, 15	10-11, 30, 38-39, 43, 84, 99, 187

Theme	Chapter(s)	Page Numbers

Bibliography

- Alison A (1853). History of Europe Volume 1. London: William Blackwood and Sons.
- Anderson F M (1791). Constitution and Selected Documents.
- Brunch TG (1947). The Seven Epistles of Christ. Washington DC USA: Review and Herald Publishing Association.
- Burke E (1790). Reflections on the Revolution in France. London: James Dodsley.
- Coffman C, Holbrook F (1989). Bible Study Guide – Present Triumph, Future Glory. Nampa USA: Pacific Press Publishing Association.
- Cooke A (2015). An Enduring Vision – Revelation Revealed. Fort Oglethorpe, USA: Teach Services Inc.
- Dalberg-Acton J, 1st Baron Acton, Ward Adolphus (2011). The Cambridge Modern History. Cambridge: Cambridge University Press.
- Devens RM (1877). Our First Century One Hundred Great Events. Springfield, USA: C A Nichols.
- Elliott EB (2015). Horae Apocalypticae. Raleigh: Lulu.com.
- Foxe J (1999). Foxe's Book of Martyrs. Grand Rapids, USA: Baker Book House.
- Froom LE (1948). Prophetic Faith of Our Fathers. Volume 2. Washington DC, USA: Review and Herald Publishing Association.
- Gaussen L (1862). The Canon of the Holy Scriptures. Part 2. Boston, USA: American Tract Society.
- Gibbon E (1997). History of the Decline and Fall of the Roman Empire. Ware, UK: Wordsworth Editions Ltd.

- Hutton WH (1908). The Age of Revolution. London: Macmillan Co.
- Jones AT (2016). Ecclesiastical Empire. California, USA: Adventist Pioneer Library.
- Melanchton P (1930s). The Augsburg Confession (The Book of Concord: The Lutheran Confessions of 1529-1580). Missouri Synod: The Lutheran Church.
- Merriam-Webster (1884). Webster's Unabridged Dictionary. New York: Harper and Brothers.
- Smith U (2006). Daniel and the Revelation. Washington DC, USA: Review and Herald Publishing Association.
- Stefanovic R (2019). Bible Study Guide on the book of Revelation. Nampa, USA: Pacific Press Publishing Association.
- Summerbell N (1878). History of the Christian Church From its Establishment by Christ to AD 1971. Cincinnati, USA: Cincinnati Christian Pulpit.
- Walther D (1968). Were the Albigenses and Waldenses Forerunners of the Reformation? Berrien Springs, USA: Andrews University Seminary Studies.
- Wilkinson BG (2013). Truth Triumphant: The Church in the Wilderness. Nampa, USA: Pacific Press Publishing Association.
- Wilkinson J (2015). Quakerism Examined. Books on Demand Ltd.
- Wylie JA (2015). The History of Protestantism. Delmarva Publications Inc.

Newspapers and Magazines:
- Blackwood's Magazine (November 1870).
- Sidney Morning Herald (12 February 2018).

- Signs of the Times (December 1987).
- The Guardian Newspaper (21 January 2013).
- The Guardian Newspaper (31 October 2017).

Websites:
- www.britannica.com/event/French-Revolution
- www.britannica.com/topic/Waldenses
- www.crystalvaults.com/crystal-encyclopedia/lapislazuli
- www.deedsofgod.com
- www.revelationbibleprophecy.org
- www.theguardian.com.uk
- www.themichigancatholic.org
- www.weekly.israelbiblecentre.com/who-were-nicolaitans
- Wikipedia – Arab-Byzantine wars
- Wikipedia – Attila the Hun
- Wikipedia – French Revolution Age of Reason

General Reading:
- KJV – King James Version of the Bible
- NKJV – New King James Version of the Bible
- NIV – New International Version of the Bible
- White EG (2006). Early Writings. Washington DC, USA.
  Review and Herald Publishing Association.
- White EG (2017). The Great Controversy between Christ and Satan.
  Nampa, USA.
  Pacific Press Publishing Association.